THE

ZEN MONKEY

AND THE

LOTUS FLOWER

✳ ✳ ✳

52 Stories to Relieve Stress, Stop Negative Thoughts, Find Happiness, and Live Your Best Life..

Daniel D'apollo

Ebook Edition

First Edition: 2023

ISBN: **9789693292770**

2

Table of Contents

A Tale of Tails and Trunks 7

Daydreams and Dragonflies 10

The Playful Tormenter and the Gentle Giant 13

The Wise Tit and the Ambitious Goose 16

The Boastful Beetle and the Gentle Giant 19

Morning Nuts and Monkey Business 23

The Sly Spearman and the Wise Deer 26

The Golden Cage 30

The Tender-Hearted Feathered King 33

The Mantis' Misstep 37

The Sly Falcon and the Wise Rooster 40

Birds of a Feather 44

The Anxious Giant 47

The Tale of Two Shepherds 50

The Tenderhearted Woodpecker and the Ungrateful King 53

The Unseen Wisdom in Waste 57

The Rumor Run 60

Buzz of Enlightenment 63

The Vanity Pool 66

The Vast Shore and the Tiny Kingdom 70

The Boozy Beak Brigade 73

The Humble Sojourner 77

The Shimmering Friend 80

The Dance of Fortune 84

A Clever Encounter 87

The Chain of Distraction 91

Monkey Business in the Royal Garden 94

The Joyful Swim 97

Sweet Lies and Sour Reality 100

A Quick Peek 103

Granny's Gentle Giant 105

The Simple Wisdom of the Wild 109

The Clever Coin-Carrying Mouse and the Stone-hearted Stonecutter
.... 112

The Humble Wanderer 114

Crafty Capers in Crocodile Cove 118

The Pea Pursuit 122

A Glimpse of Gold and Feathers 125

The Sly Arbitrator 129

A Wingbeat in the Wild 133

The Deer King's Gift 136

The Unexpected Reflections 140

The Chatty Voyager 143

The Timely Rescue 146

The Chronicles of Unlikely Friendship 149

Flight Lessons 152

A Speck in the Cosmos 155

A Cave Tale in the Pouring Rain 158

The Little Builders and the Big Questions 161

A Tale of Two Fawns 164

The Mighty Heart of True Happiness 167

The Crafty Sage and the Wise Rats 171

The Ape's Heartfelt Rescue 175

Conclusion 178

Forward

Hey there, Reader!

Welcome to "The Zen Monkey and The Lotus Flower"! Inside, you'll find magical stories, each one filled with secrets to discover and lessons to learn.

Think of this book as a special friend, always ready to share a new story every week for a whole year. These tales are all about being kind, enjoying each tiny moment, and finding the magic in letting things be.

Every story is like a small drop of rain, making ripples in a pond, showing you something new or reminding you of an old truth. Some might make you smile, while others get you thinking. No matter the story, each one has its own magic waiting just for you.

You don't need to know anything about Buddhism to enjoy these stories. They're for everyone, no matter where you come from. They're little keys that can open big doors to new ideas and ways of looking at the world.

Now, there's a word you might come across: "dharma." It's a special word in Buddhism, talking about life's big truths and how things work.

As you read each page, I hope these stories light up something inside you, showing you all the love, joy, and wisdom, you carry in your heart. I wish for this book to be like a sparkly guide, reminding you of the amazing things you've always had inside.

Ready to start our adventure? Let's dive into a world where each story whispers a secret, guiding us to a life full of love, wonder, and understanding.

A Tale of Tails and Trunks

Once upon a time, in the vibrant city of Varanasi, the local king adored his array of elephants. Among them, one particularly stood out - not just for its might but for its unique companion, a little stray dog. The dog initially came around for the morsels of rice that dropped from the elephant's mouth, but with time, their acquaintance blossomed into a beautiful friendship. The duo became inseparable; the dog would sleep curled by the elephant's foot, share bath time, and engage in playful antics, with the elephant joyfully swinging the dog with her trunk. They shared their meals together, and it became such that the elephant refused to eat unless her furry friend was by her side.

However, one day, fate took a harsh turn when an ill-tempered stable hand, drawn by a fleeting opportunity to make some quick money, sold the dog to a passing peasant. The absence of her companion left the elephant in utter despair. She became a shadow of her former lively self, refusing to eat, drink, or partake in her daily routines, and stood morosely in her stall, swaying from side to side, lost in the memories of the joyful times she shared with her friend.

The king, worried by the declining health and spirits of his favorite elephant, summoned his wise adviser to diagnose the problem. The adviser, after a thorough examination, concluded that the elephant was physically fine, indicating an emotional distress was at play. On inquiring with the elephant's caretaker, he discovered the recent loss of the dog which seemed to have cast a deep emotional scar on the elephant.

The adviser relayed his findings to the king, who felt helpless initially at the daunting task of finding a single dog in the vast city. However, the adviser concocted a smart plan. He suggested issuing a royal decree stating a hefty fine would be levied on anyone found harboring the dog from the royal stables. The proclamation did the trick, as the scared peasant swiftly set the dog free, who, without missing a beat, sprinted back to the royal stables and to his beloved friend.

The reunion was a sight to behold; the elephant, tears rolling down her cheeks, delicately cradled her furry friend with her trunk, expressing a joy that words could not. The duo relished their meal together once again, marking the end of the melancholic days. The elephant perked up, and their playful, carefree days resumed, proving yet again, that the essence of friendship holds the power to heal and rejuvenate spirits, be it of humans or animals.

Lessons:

The narrative depicts a touching saga that highlights the virtues of loyalty, friendship, and the emotional depth and capacity for love shared by all beings, whether on two legs or four. It subtly moves us to acknowledge and appreciate the unspoken bonds of camaraderie and love that enrich our lives. Amidst the modern-day hustle, where relationships often take a backseat, this tale is a gentle reminder to honor and cherish the beautiful connections we have, for they hold the power to heal, comfort and bring joy in the most unassuming ways. In a world driven by material pursuits, the essence of pure, unadulterated friendship is a treasure to hold onto.

2

Daydreams and Dragonflies

Once in a small village, there lived a boy named Soft Chimney. He loved playing in the nearby woods. One morning, he picked up a stick pretending it to be his sword and a bigger one as his make-believe horse. He ran through the woods until he was out of breath. Dropping his sticks, he saw a beautiful butterfly hopping from one flower to another.

Soft Chimney began chasing the butterfly, laughing and running around. The butterfly flew up and landed on his finger before flying off again. Tired from all the playing, Soft Chimney lay down on a bed of pine needles for a nap.

He dreamed he was the butterfly, flying from flower to flower, enjoying the sweet taste of nectar. When he woke up, a strange thought crossed his mind. Was he a boy dreaming of being a butterfly, or a butterfly dreaming of being a boy? After thinking for a bit, he decided it didn't matter. Whether a boy or a butterfly, there was so much to see and enjoy. He ran off to continue playing, his heart light.

Lessons:

The story of Soft Chimney invites us to look at life with a fresh, playful perspective. In our adult lives, we often get caught up in the race to get ahead, forgetting the simple joy of living in the moment.

Much like Soft Chimney, every one of us can take a break from our daily grind to enjoy what's around us. Whether it's the joy of watching a butterfly, the wind rustling through the trees, or the simple pleasure of a good meal, life offers small moments of happiness every day.

In today's fast-paced world, we can sometimes feel like we're losing touch with the simple, beautiful moments that make life enjoyable. The curiosity and joy of Soft Chimney remind us that it's important to take a step back, appreciate what we have, and enjoy the world around us. The playful exploration in the story encourages us to keep a curious and open mind, to not get too caught up in the serious, and to find joy in the simple things life offers.

3

The Playful Tormenter and the Gentle Giant

Once upon a time, in a lavish forest near the city of Gaya in northeastern India, a powerful buffalo roamed. His presence was monumental—muscular frame and grand horns with sharp ends, resembling a majestic mountain on the move. Although feared by lions and tigers for his might, the buffalo carried a heart full of gentleness and wisdom.

Among the forest dwellers, a mischievous monkey discovered the buffalo's temperament and saw an opportunity for amusement at the buffalo's expense. He'd play tricks, ride on the buffalo's back, swing between his horns, cover his eyes, and startle him awake from peaceful slumbers. Regardless of the monkey's antics, the buffalo remained undisturbed, embracing a calm demeanor.

An observant owl, puzzled by their interaction, once asked the buffalo why he allowed such antics. The buffalo shared that it's easy to show patience towards the kind, but the true test lies in showing patience towards those who seek to disturb your peace. Through enduring the monkey's mischief, he was growing in tolerance and compassion, hoping his demeanor might inspire change in his playful tormenter.

The owl, touched by the buffalo's insight, thanked him for unveiling a profound perspective, soaring back to her treetop abode with newfound wisdom.

Lessons:
Reflecting on this tale, we delve into the essence of patience, tolerance, and the practice of gentle assertiveness amid provocation. In a world where immediate reactions are often sought and celebrated, the buffalo's restraint invites us to question our impulses, especially when faced with minor annoyances or deliberate provocations.

We are living in times where social media and instant communications often serve as platforms for unfiltered reactions, creating a cycle of negativity and stress. The monkey in the story could represent these modern-day irritants that test our patience daily. On the other hand, the composed response of the buffalo encourages us to take a step back, breathe, and choose our battles wisely.

The narrative here similarly invites us to foster a culture of understanding, patience, and thoughtfulness, much needed in our fast-paced world. Each interaction, no matter how trivial or testing, offers an opportunity for personal growth and the spread of compassion—a gentle reminder that patience isn't a sign of weakness, but a reflection of inner strength and maturity.

4
The Wise Tit and the Ambitious Goose

Once upon a time in a peaceful countryside, a wise old sage and his curious student, Porridge Knees, were strolling along the edge of a serene swamp. As they strolled, Porridge Knees was awestruck by a large flock of geese elegantly soaring through the sky.

"Master, behold the geese," said Porridge Knees with a tinge of envy, "They will traverse thousands of miles, gaining a grand view of the world beneath. Their knowledge and experience must be boundless!"

The sage, with a gentle smile, pointed towards a humble marsh tit, who was joyfully hopping from reed to reed along the marsh's edge. The small bird seemed so content, fluttering around in her little haven, fetching her modest meal amidst the reeds, unbothered by the vast skies above.

"You see, Porridge Knees," the sage gently explained, "While the geese chase horizons seeking enlightenment from the vastness, our little marsh tit finds her joy right here in the familiar. She ventures not into the distant skies but finds all she needs amidst these humble reeds. She's free from the shackles of relentless quest. There's a simple yet profound contentment in appreciating what's right in front of us. I'd rather embody the essence of this modest marsh tit than the ambitious goose."

Lessons:

The tale gently leads us towards understanding that life's contentment isn't necessarily found in relentless pursuits or distant horizons. Just like the swamp, finding joy in the familiar, cherishing the immediate surroundings, and appreciating the present moment could lead to a fulfilling existence.

In a world where ambition drives many to seek constantly beyond the horizon, this story invites us to pause and reflect. The modern pursuit—be it for wealth, status, or adventure—often mirrors the flight of the ambitious goose, overlooking the simple yet enriching experiences available right where we are. The charm of a simple life, akin to the swamp tit's, is a narrative less told, yet potentially equally, if not more, rewarding. Through embracing the present, nurturing gratitude for the immediate, and cherishing the modesty of the 'here and now,' there lies a path toward genuine contentment and meaningful life.

5
The Boastful Beetle and the Gentle Giant

Once upon a time, nestled between two old-fashioned Indian towns, there was a charming riverside inn. It was the kind of place where weary travelers would pause, refresh, and share stories of the road. Often, they'd sit under the open sky, enjoying a cool evening breeze, sipping on hearty brews. On one such evening, amidst laughter and tales, a traveler's beer spilled, its amber liquid finding a home in a rock's hollow cradle.

Now, not far from this jovial scene, a dung beetle was embarking on his daily quest towards the river, guided by the rustic scent of the travelers' animals. Our little beetle stumbled upon the wayward beer and, enticed, took a sip, then another, and before he knew it, he was drunk on the effervescent brew.

Feeling the world sway under his tiny legs, the beetle made his way to the riverbank, tripping over a mound of droppings and mud. Upon finally standing upright, though shaky and smeared in mud, he thought, "Ah, such might I possess, the world trembles under my huge presence!"

At that very moment, an elephant was ambling towards the river for a drink. Observing the ridiculous display of the beetle, the elephant decided to tread another path to avoid disturbing the tiny creature. But the beetle saw this and, with all the bravado of a knight, called out, "Ah, you flee, mighty creature! Scared of my prowess, are you? Face me!"

The elephant, seeing through the drunken daze of the beetle, thought of imparting a lesson in humility. He answered, "Very well, Mr. Beetle, I accept your bold challenge, and I shall choose our battleground."

With a swift motion, the elephant turned, lifted his tail, and with a gentle thud, enveloped the beetle in a warm mound of dung. "Ah, you seem right at home, Mr. Beetle," chuckled the elephant, "I hereby claim my humble victory." He then continued his peaceful journey to the river, quenched his thirst, and ambled back into the serene woods, leaving the beetle to contemplate his deeds under the warm, earthen mound.

Lessons:

The story of the beetle and the elephant shows us the importance of staying humble and recognizing our limitations. The beetle, after having a bit too much to drink, believed he was stronger than an elephant, a notion that quickly landed him in trouble. On the other hand, the elephant, despite being immensely stronger, chose a humble approach to teach the beetle a lesson, without causing any real harm.

In our world today, it's easy to get carried away with our importance, especially on social media or in competitive workplaces. This story suggests that being humble and respecting others, regardless of their status or size, is a valuable approach. It also teaches us that it's okay to accept our mistakes and learn from them rather than continue on a path of delusion or arrogance.

Additionally, the elephant's choice to humor the beetle's challenge, instead of reacting angrily or with violence, can be a reminder in our daily interactions. It encourages dealing with disagreements or conflicts in a kind, understanding manner. And just like the elephant, sometimes taking a gentle, light-hearted

approach can make a situation better and leave room for everyone to learn and grow from the experience.

6

Morning Nuts and Monkey Business

Once upon a time, in a serene little town, there lived a wise old sage who enjoyed imparting life's teachings to his curious pupils. One fine morning, with the sun painting a warm glow in the sky, the sage took his pupils on an outing to the local zoo owned by the king. They arrived just as the zookeeper was starting his day feeding the animals.

As they approached the monkey enclosure, they overheard the zookeeper telling the monkeys, "My furry buddies, I have some fine chestnuts for you today. I'll give each of you three chestnuts now, and four more this evening."

The monkeys immediately erupted into a cacophony of protest, shrieking and bouncing all around. "Only three now? That's unfair!" they seemed to be saying in their own monkey way.

The zookeeper, trying to keep the peace, quickly reconsidered. "Okay, okay," he said, relenting. "I'll give each of you four chestnuts now, and three more this evening."

Suddenly, all was well. The monkeys happily accepted their chestnuts, chattering and munching away contentedly. They were now in agreement that fairness had been restored.

The students watched this spectacle, bewildered. But the sage, with a gentle smile, turned to them and said, "Sometimes, fairness is more about perception than reality. It's about seeing things in a way that brings contentment."

Lessons:

In today's fast-paced world, the clamor for fairness often resembles the monkey's initial outrage, swift and loud. Yet, as the zookeeper's simple solution demonstrated, sometimes a slight shift in perspective can restore harmony. Our understanding of fairness can be very subjective, swayed by emotion rather than logic. The search for fairness, be it in our workplaces or our communities, might sometimes require a step back and a fresh outlook, much like the one offered by the sage. This doesn't mean compromising our values, but rather opening up to different ways of looking at a situation.

It reminds us too of the gentle narratives of Charlie Mackesy, where acceptance and understanding reign over quick judgments. Thích Nhất Hạnh's teachings also nudge us towards such inner reflections, paving a path towards a peaceful coexistence amidst the apparent disparities life throws our way. Through these lenses, we might find that what we perceive as unfair might just be a call for a broader understanding and a tender open-heartedness toward life's unfolding scenario.

7

The Sly Spearman and the Wise Deer

Once, not far from the bustling city of Varanasi, nestled amidst a verdant forest, lived a graceful antelope. She thrived on the bounties that fell from the trees, keeping to a peaceful existence. In stark contrast, a hunter inhabited the same woodland, whose livelihood depended on slaying the forest's denizens.

With clever schemes, the hunter devised a plan. He built a hidden platform high in the trees, hoping to ambush animals when they came for the fruits below. The crafty man chose a tree that seemed to be a regular feeding spot for the antelope. After setting his snare up high, the hunter discreetly waited for his prey.

Early the next morning, concealed on his perch, he patiently awaited his chance. Before long, the antelope arrived, charmed by the sweet fruits of the tree as she had been for years. But today was different. A faint whiff of danger tingled her senses - a subtle scent of a human.

Frozen in her tracks, the antelope's instincts told her something was amiss. The hunter, restless for his prize, sought to lure her closer. He gently tossed some fruits towards her. However, this unusual action rang alarm bells for the antelope. The game was up.

She decided to humor the hunter's attempt, addressing the tree loudly, "Oh grand tree, your fruits seem to act against nature today, flying out to greet me and in threes, with no wind to justify it! Since you've abandoned your usual ways, I shall seek another tree that stays true to its nature." And with that, she began to trot away.

The hunter, fuming at this mockery, revealed himself, hurling his spear in frustration, but the antelope was far out of reach. His threats echoed through the forest as she elegantly evaded his malicious intent.

As she made her way to safer grounds, she left the hunter with a piece of her wisdom, "Perhaps, hunter, it's time to reconsider this perilous path you tread. Those who seek to harm the gentle beings of the forest with deceit might find fate's cruel spear aimed at their hearts someday. Reflect upon today."

Lessons:

The story illustrates the profound teachings of awareness, integrity, and the consequences of our actions. The antelope's heightened senses and the hunter's failed deceit remind us of the importance of being alert and honest, not just with others but also with ourselves. The hunter's frustration, ignited by his failed deception, speaks volumes about how impulsive actions driven by anger can lead to failure. Meanwhile, the antelope's grace and composed departure embody a lesson in maintaining dignity and wisdom, even when faced with deceit or danger.

In today's fast-paced world, we often overlook the simplicity of honesty and the rewards of patience. Our impatience may sometimes drive us to adopt deceitful tactics for quick gains, mirroring the hunter's actions. The story invites us to reflect on the repercussions of such behaviors, suggesting a life led with awareness and integrity is far more rewarding and less perilous.

Drawing from this tale, we can aspire to be more like the antelope - discerning, patient, and wise in our dealings, avoiding the path of deceit that only leads to a hollow victory or, worse, a bitter failure. Our modern endeavors, be it personal or professional, beckon us to embody these virtues, building a foundation of trust, patience, and integrity that would only steer us towards a more wholesome and meaningful existence.

8

The Golden Cage

Once, in a bustling town, a wise old man and his curious pupil,
named Falling Barnacle, strolled through a lively marketplace. As
they navigated through the crowd, Falling Barnacle was
captivated by a pheasant held in a cramped bamboo cage, its
feathers shimmering under the sun.

"This bird is astonishing," he exclaimed, eyes wide in wonder.

"Yes," the wise old man nodded. "Its beauty might catch the eye
of the king, who might decide to keep it in a golden cage, feeding

it the choicest grains and freshest water. Yet, in the wild, this bird would toil from dawn to dusk, scratching the earth for seeds, and travel far for a sip of water. Despite the struggle, the pheasant would choose that life over a gilded cage."

The image of a golden cage is dazzling, yet it's a cage nonetheless. The old man's words emphasized a straightforward yet profound truth, the essence of freedom over comfort. This story reminds us to reflect on our own lives. How often do we trade our freedom for comfort, our autonomy for a gilded cage of luxury?

In a modern context, this could manifest in many ways - sticking to a monotonous job for the sake of financial security, clinging to a stagnant relationship for fear of loneliness, or adhering to societal norms and expectations at the cost of our true desires. The allure of a "golden cage" is a powerful one, yet, the essence of life lies in the freedom to explore, to make choices, and to grow, even if it means facing adversities.

Lessons:

The tale reminds adults to evaluate the cages we confine ourselves to, some gilded with pretenses of comfort. The humble pheasant teaches us to cherish our freedom, urging us to step out of our comfort zones and embrace the raw, often challenging, yet fulfilling realm of autonomy. As Thich Nhat Hanh often speaks of mindfulness and living authentically, this story echoes a similar sentiment. Much like Charlie Mackesy's narrative of embracing life with all its ups and downs, the tale of the pheasant encourages us to seek a life of meaning, even if it comes with scratches from digging the earth and miles to walk for a sip of water.

9
The Tender-Hearted Feathered King

Once upon a time, in the serene meadows of north-central India, there existed a delightful community of parakeets. They made their home atop a hill, nestled within the comforting embrace of silk cotton trees. The community was led by a wise king and queen, who were parents to a charming son. With the grace of time, the young one's plumage blossomed into colors more splendid, and his form, ever more graceful.

As the sun cast longer shadows, marking the fatigue of age on the king and queen, they knew it was time for their son to wear the crown. They beckoned him, expressing their wish for him to lead their cherished flock to lands abundant with nourishment. With a heart brimming with love and honor, the young king accepted, promising to shelter them as they had, him.

Just beyond the hill, lay vast expanses of verdant fields, a realm under a wealthy landowner. His fields were a quilt of paddy, painting the earth in shades of promising green. Among these, a patch at the hill's base beckoned the young feathered king. Observing the ripe grains, he led his flock there to feast. However, the guardian of this patch, employed by the landowner, was less than pleased with the birds' feast amidst his charge. Though he tried to shoo them away, they merely fluttered to another corner, continuing their banquet.

He observed an unusual sight - the young king, after sating his hunger, collected a beak full of grains and soared skywards. This piqued the guardian's worry, making him rush to the landowner, fearing blame for the loss of grains. The landowner, rather than expressing anger, was intrigued by the tale of the altruistic parakeet and wished to witness this sight himself. He instructed the guardian to capture the benevolent bird alive.

The following dawn brought the feathered king and his flock back to the fields. But fate had a snare laid in wait. As the trap encircled his leg, the king thought of his flock first, choosing silence over an alarming cry, letting them finish their meal. Once satiated, he let out a cry, sending them fluttering away, leaving him in the trap's clutches.

The guardian, recognizing the cry of distress, hurried to the site, overjoyed at capturing the very bird as instructed. He carried the captured king to the landowner who, upon meeting the bird, inquired about his unusual endeavor. With a voice carrying notes of kindness, the bird shared his tale - it was a simple act of love, an homage to the elderly who had nurtured him. His beak carried not just grains but an earnest duty towards his aging parents.

Lessons:

The tale stirred the heart of the landowner, revealing before him a mirror of values long forgotten. He admired the bird's noble heart, let him loose, and extended his fields as a gesture to the bird's indomitable spirit of care and duty. The experience was akin to a leaf rustling softly, reminding the landowner of the tender cords of care, duty, and respect that bound lives together, be it the lives of humans or birds.

The world continues to rush past, often overlooking the gentleness of actions rooted in love, respect, and duty. The story unfolds a simple truth, in the grand scheme of things, it's the humble, sincere acts that echo the loudest, teaching the essence of being human. And in the fast pace of modern life, the simplicity and sincerity behind such acts are often overlooked or forgotten. Just as the young parakeet king's duty to his parents highlighted the innate virtue of caring, it's a gentle reminder to humankind to hold onto the basics of love, respect, and duty, even when the world around us evolves rapidly.

This gentle story tells adults to pause amidst their hectic schedules and reflect on the foundational values that make life more meaningful. It's not the grandiose gestures but the small, thoughtful actions driven by love and duty that create ripples of change. In a world that's constantly racing ahead, embracing the simple yet profound virtues of compassion, respect, and duty, much like the tender-hearted feathered king, could lead us toward a more harmonious existence.

This tale encourages us to find wisdom in simplicity, to cultivate a heart that cares unconditionally, and to uphold a sense of duty that transcends the ordinary, propelling us towards extraordinary acts of love and kindness. The teachings embedded in this humble narrative resonate with timeless wisdom, urging the modern world to rediscover and celebrate the profound simplicity of life, rekindling a spirit of compassion and duty amidst the chaos of the contemporary world.

The Mantis' Misstep

Once upon a time, in a distant land, there was a wise sage and his diligent students who were on a long journey to a bustling city. They tread along the edge of a busy highway, amidst a chaotic dance of horses, carts, and carriages. One sunny morning, as they made their way, the student leading the group paused to observe a praying mantis attempting to cross the road.

Just at that moment, a speeding chariot approached, the horses neighing loudly, and the wheels stirring up a whirlwind of dust.

Instead of flying away to safety, the mantis, perhaps in a surge of defiance, stood on its hind legs and started waving its tiny front legs at the oncoming chariot. It was a sight that tickled a faint smile on the student's face, yet also pulled at his heartstrings. The inevitable happened in a blink; the mantis was crushed under the iron-clad wheels of the chariot, its tiny brave act ending in a moment of misfortune.

They continued on their journey, but the sage, noticing the contemplative faces of his students, decided to share his thoughts. "Sometimes, a little overconfidence can cloud our judgment, making us forget the real extent of our abilities. It's essential to know our limits, yet also strive to expand them in a wise and cautious manner," he mused as they walked along.

Lessons:

In our world today, where competition and proving oneself seem to be the driving forces, this tale reverberates with a subtle but potent message. It's easy to get swept up in the storm of proving our mettle, often overestimating our capacities. However, understanding our limits is not a sign of weakness, but a step towards wisdom. It's about embracing our capabilities and working on expanding them, rather than recklessly plunging into situations that can lead to unfortunate outcomes.

While bravery and assertiveness are valuable, they should walk hand in hand with a realistic understanding of our strengths and weaknesses. Like the mantis, a burst of overconfidence can lead to dire situations, but with a dash of humility and a spoonful of awareness, we navigate through life's highway with fewer bumps and much more grace.

11

The Sly Falcon and the Wise Rooster

Once upon a time in a place known as Bamboo Grove near Rajgir in northeastern India, a community of wildfowl enjoyed their peaceful days. They relished the warmth of the sun and scoured the lush meadows and forest floors for their daily meals. Life was good until a menacing falcon moved into their territory. He was swift and fierce, diving down from the skies, capturing a fowl, and making it his meal. Soon, the cheerful flock dwindled to half, fear reigning over the once joyful community.

Recognizing the peril, the wise rooster, their leader, took matters into his wings. He guided the remaining members of his flock to the safety of the dense bamboo grove, where the thick stalks and leaves acted as a shield against the falcon's deadly swoops. The strategy worked; the falcon couldn't navigate through the dense grove, and the birds were safe as long as they stayed within.

The falcon, although ferocious, had a keen mind. He admired the rooster's leadership and hatched a plan to lure him out into the open, hoping to make a meal out of him and later, the rest of the flock.

One fine day, the falcon approached the grove, perched on a nearby branch, and spoke to the rooster, "Noble fowl, I've been in awe of your leadership and the unity of your flock. Let's put past differences behind us. I know a place nearby filled with delicious seeds. Come, let's feast together as friends."

The rooster, unyielding, responded, "Oh, mighty hunter, friendship between us is a far-fetched tale. I've no intention of dining with you."

The falcon insisted, claiming to have changed his predatory ways, pleading for a chance to prove his newfound camaraderie.

However, the rooster had a wealth of life lessons under his feathers. He retorted, "I've learned to be wary of deceitful words, self-serving actions, and those who change colors faster than the sky at dusk. It's the actions carried in silence that speak the truth, not honeyed words. We've enough sustenance here in our haven. We need not venture out and gamble with the unknown, risking lives at the mercy of false promises."

The falcon, realizing the rooster's wisdom was a wall too high to fly over, spread his wings and soared away, searching for less discerning prey in faraway lands.

Lessons:

The life of the rooster and his flock is a humble reminder of the essence of wise leadership, loyalty, and the ability to see through false promises, even when masked with sweet words. In today's world, where change is as constant as the northern star, discerning the truth from a guise becomes vital. Much like the rooster, we must recognize when to step into the unknown and when to find contentment in our current circumstances, ensuring the safety and wellbeing of not just ourselves, but our community as a whole.

Moreover, the tale subtly tells us to value the simple yet profound act of vigilance and prudent decision-making, especially when faced with tempting propositions. Just as the rooster prioritized the safety of his flock over a tempting offer, we too should uphold integrity and wisdom, navigating through the complex, often misleading narratives that cross our paths today.

12

Birds of a Feather

Once upon a time, in a serene countryside, a wise sage and his curious pupil, named Royal Worm, were strolling near an attractive lake. The fresh morning air was filled with the subtle fragrance of blooming flowers, but Royal Worm seemed to have something else on his mind. Breaking the silence, he inquired, "Master, how might I strive to be a noteworthy individual?"

At that precise moment, a scene unfolded before them that captured the essence of his inquiry. A swift hawk plunged from the sky, gracefully swooping over the calm waters where a serene egret stood, patiently awaiting his catch on slender legs. It was a scene that seemed to blend the urgency of action with the patience of waiting.

Without taking his eyes off the scene, the sage offered, "See, the hawk doesn't endeavor to sharpen its sight to be an exceptional hunter, nor does the egret stretch its legs daily to be a remarkable fisher. They simply are as nature intended. Similarly, Royal Worm, greatness isn't an attire one puts on; it's an inherent cloth we're cut from. The endeavor isn't to become, but to realize and embrace what one already is."

Lessons:

Today, this slice of wisdom holds a mirror to our incessant pursuit of becoming 'someone.' Amid the rat races, we often forget the essence of being, the unique blend of qualities we naturally embody. Like the hawk and egret, our inherent strengths and attributes carve our niche. It isn't about molding ourselves into the shoes of societal expectations but recognizing and nurturing our inherent potential.

The story reminds adults to veer from the constant quest of becoming and to dive into the journey of self-discovery. It's in the latter where the spirit finds a playground to dance to the rhythm of authenticity. As we move amidst the daily whirlwinds, this tale is a reminder to pause, reflect, and embrace the unadulterated essence that propels us toward our unique greatness, much like the effortless ease of the hawk's swoop and the egret's patience.

13

The Anxious Giant

Once, nestled in the comforting veil of a forest near a sprawling Indian kingdom, lived a magnificent elephant. She was a giant, yet gentle soul, with a hide almost white, blending with the soft morning mist. She cherished the rhythmic days spent with her herd, amidst the orchestra of whispers between leaves and the ancient wisdom rooted in the forest.

But one day, her idyllic world was shattered as the king's elephant trainers, enchanted by her majestic size and grace, decided to capture her for the royal parade. The unsettling storm of human presence alarmed her, as she was roped and dragged into a prison of logs, her freedom snatched away like leaves in a whirlwind.

The trainers, unaware of the scars their actions left on her heart, relentlessly tried to tame her spirit through fear. With every prod and shout, she trembled and panicked, unable to comprehend the sudden darkness clouding her world. The ordeal whipped up a storm of terror in her heart, which one day broke the bounds of her prison, as she sprinted towards the unseen embrace of the Himalayas.

In her frantic escape, she found solitude amidst the towering peaks and whispering streams, far away from the clutches of men. Yet, the ghost of fear followed her, as even the rustle of leaves or the murmur of the wind sent shivers down her spine, throwing her into a whirlpool of panic.

In the silent witness of the mountains, lived a perceptive owl, who saw the giant's endless ordeal against phantom fears. One fine dawn, the owl decided to gift the gentle giant a mirror to her fears. As the owl approached her and assured her of the benign surroundings, she listened, her ears tuning to the symphony of truth in the owl's words.

The elephant realized the chains of fear were her creation, a harsh melody she had unconsciously tuned her heart to. With patience and gentle talks of courage from her own heart, she began to unravel the ropes of panic, replacing them with strings of understanding and love for the music of life around her.

Lessons:

Through this tale, a soft reminder echoes across our modern lives that are often encased in fears, and self-made barriers against imagined adversities. Much like the elephant, we might find ourselves entrapped in a whirlpool of anxieties, where the rustle of uncertainties sends us into spirals of dread. Yet, if we take a pause, tune our hearts to the whispers of understanding, and face our fears with the gentle eye of awareness, we might just find the melody of life that has always been playing around us, waiting to be heard.

The way forward is not in running away from what scares us but facing them with a curious heart, a patient mind, and the willingness to understand that often, the ghosts we run from are the ones we create. Like the gentle giant, let's strive to listen, understand, and dance to the symphony of life, unshackled by fears.

14

The Tale of Two Shepherds

Once upon a time in a modest village, lived two young girls named Ellie and Anna. They were bestowed with the duty of shepherding a sheep each, to ensure its safety for the sake of the wool that would later be traded at the market to aid their families.

Ellie had a knack for knowledge. She would often borrow books from the local school teacher to quench her thirst for learning. One fine day, she led her sheep to the grassy plains, found a comfy spot under a tree, and delved into a new book she had borrowed. The pages of the book swept her away to a far-off land, making her oblivious to the passing of time and her sheep that now had strayed away. When she finally snapped back to reality, her sheep was nowhere in sight. Despite her relentless search, the sheep remained lost.

On the other hand, Anna was more inclined towards the sweet delights of life. She too, led her sheep to the meadow, but soon sneaked back to the village with her pals on a quest for honey. As the sun started to dip below the horizon, she returned to the meadow only to find her sheep had vanished. No matter where she looked, her sheep was nowhere to be found.

Lessons:

The tale of Ellie and Anna reflects an essential understanding, regardless of Ellie's studious nature and Anna's sweet-toothed adventures, the result was a loss that their families endured equally. It illustrates that our actions, irrespective of the motives behind them, can have ramifications on others around us. In our modern-day scenario, this could relate to myriad aspects of adult life. Whether it be getting engulfed in work and neglecting family or pursuing personal desires at the expense of others' needs, the outcomes affect not just us, but those dependent or connected to us.

The essence of mindfulness in our actions and balancing our pursuits with our responsibilities is subtly echoed through this narrative. It pushes us to acknowledge that while chasing our aspirations or indulging in pleasures, keeping an awareness of our surroundings and the impact of our actions on others is quintessential. It might not always require monumental shifts, but small tweaks in our daily endeavors to ensure we aren't causing inadvertent harm or neglect towards others.

15

The Tenderhearted Woodpecker and the Ungrateful King

Once in the green regions of northwest India, there existed a peculiar woodpecker known for two distinctive traits - his captivating appearance and his unusual dietary preference. Unlike his kin who relished insects and worms, this woodpecker found satisfaction in the young tendrils of plants, blooms, and fruits, driven by his reluctance to harm another being. His compassion was a well-known tale among the forest folk, always extended to anyone in distress.

One fine morning, as the woodpecker soared through the canopy, he stumbled upon a sound of distress emanating from below. Descending, he discovered a lion, the proclaimed monarch of the woods, writhing in discomfort. "Oh mighty one," the woodpecker inquired, "what calamity has befallen you? Is it a poisoned arrow or a lurking illness?" The lion, with labored breath, explained, "Oh gentle bird, I am neither poisoned nor ill. A stubborn bone has lodged itself in my throat, choking the life out of me. It neither advances nor retreats, and I fear this might be the end of me. Can you lend your aid?"

The woodpecker, after brief contemplation, devised a plan. Fetching a stout stick, he requested the lion to open his mouth wide, upon which he wedged the stick between the lion's teeth, keeping the ferocious jaw agape. With delicate courage, he ventured into the lion's throat, dislodging the bone bit by bit, until it was free. The bone was carried out in his beak, and as he removed the stick, the lion's breath of relief echoed through the forest. A succinct thanks was given, and the lion retreated to recuperate, while the woodpecker resumed his search for daily sustenance.

However, fate was not as kind in the months to follow. The anticipated rains betrayed the land, plunging it into a cruel drought. The once lush foliage now bore no fruit or flower. The woodpecker's strength dwindled with each passing day of fruitless search for food. It was on one such frail flight he spotted the lion he once saved, now feasting upon an antelope. Driven by desperate hunger, the woodpecker approached the lion, hoping for a share. But as he humbly paced near the lion, awaiting recognition, none came. Overcome by desperation, the woodpecker reminded the lion of their past encounter, only to be met with scorn. "You were but fortunate to enter a lion's jaws and live. Consider that your reward and vanish before you join my feast," snarled the lion.

Hurt but not angered, the woodpecker perched on a nearby tree where an owl sat, having witnessed the ordeal. The owl urged vengeance, to which the woodpecker replied, "It's not my place to punish. My aid was an act of compassion, not a loan to be repaid." The owl admired the woodpecker's wisdom and humility. With a heavy heart yet free of malice, the woodpecker flew in pursuit of sustenance elsewhere.

Lessons:

In reviewing this tale, the gentle dance of virtues like compassion, gratitude, and humility against the rough edges of ingratitude and entitlement becomes apparent. Each encounter in life, much like the woodpecker's, often bears the seed of a lesson or a reflection of one's inner landscape. In a world rapidly veering towards individualism and immediate gratification, the essence of unconditional aid and the grace of humility can become the balm that fosters connection and understanding amidst adversity. While it's natural to expect gratitude, anchoring actions in intrinsic goodness can sometimes lead to self-discovery and peace that outlasts fleeting acknowledgments.

16

The Unseen Wisdom in Waste

Once upon a time, in a quiet village, lived a wise old sage known for his profound understanding of life and nature. One fine morning, as the mist gently lifted off the ground, he decided to take a stroll alongside his earnest student, Limber Log.

During their walk amidst the freshness of the dawn, Limber Log couldn't help but seek some insight. He turned to the sage and asked, "Master, where should one look to uncover the profound truths of life?"

The sage, with a calm smile, gently directed, "Look towards the grass beneath your feet, Limber Log."

Limber Log was puzzled, "So low?" he questioned.

Without a pause, the sage extended his view, "Now, observe the soil beneath the grass."

"Even lower?" Limber Log was now utterly bemused.

The sage chuckled softly, "Now, pay attention to the ant crawling within the soil."

"Surely, not that low!" Limber Log expressed his disbelief.

Unperturbed, the sage calmly spoke, "Now, notice the waste left behind by the ant."

"Oh, not that low!" Limber Log was almost distraught now.

Yet, the sage with a smile of serene knowing, queried, "Why not that low? Understand that even the waste, something deemed insignificant, holds a vital place in the circle of life. Without such small acts of nature, the circle would remain incomplete, disrupting our very existence."

Lessons:

The simplicity of this conversation reflects a profound reality. Often, we look for significance in the grand, the obvious, and the eye-catching, disregarding the humble and the mundane. Yet, it's in the unseen, overlooked details where often the essence of existence and perhaps the truth we seek resides.

As we navigate through the fast-paced modern life, laden with ambitions, it's easy to overlook the basic yet essential elements that hold our existence together. The story subtly tells us to acknowledge the unsung aspects of our life, the unnoticed, the unappreciated, and yet, the indispensable.

Like the sage enlightened Limber Log, it might do us well to pause, reflect, and appreciate the simple processes and elements that construct our life's foundation. In recognizing and respecting the simplicity around us, we open doors to a deeper understanding and a more harmonious existence amidst the complexities of the modern world.

17 The Rumor Run

17

The Rumor Run

Once upon a time, nestled in the countryside outside Mumbai, there was a curious rabbit. His humble abode was rooted in a lush patch near a towering palm tree. One breezy afternoon, after a hearty meal, he lounged beside his home, lost in thoughts. "What would become of me if the earth were to shatter into pieces?" he pondered. As fate would have it, a heavy coconut plummeted from a tree, crashing onto a leaf, echoing a thud that vibrated through the ground. Startled, the rabbit jumped to his feet, "The earth is crumbling!" he cried out, fear lacing his voice. Without a second glance, he sprinted away.

60

As he raced through the woods, another rabbit scurried beside him, questioning his frantic run. "The earth is falling apart! Run!" Our worried rabbit exclaimed, passing on his fear. Word spread like wildfire amongst the forest folk, and soon, a myriad of animals joined this frenzied race toward the unknown. The deer, the boars, the buffalo, and even an elephant, and a rhinoceros joined the brigade, their thumping feet resonating through the ground, a rhythmic beat of dread.

Perched on a hill, a wise old lion heard the reverberations. Curiosity drew him out, and upon seeing the spectacle of panic-stricken animals, he positioned himself bravely before the onrushing herd, letting out three deep roars that echoed through the trees, halting the herd in their tracks.

The inquisitive lion, desiring to uncover the root of this mass hysteria, engaged with an elephant who muttered, "The earth is ending!" When questioned further, a chain of blame unraveled - from elephant to buffalo, from buffalo to deer, and from deer to rabbit. Eventually, the lion was led to our original panicked rabbit who narrated his tale of the terrifying sound that led to his flight.

With a blend of skepticism and wisdom, the lion decided to investigate the matter firsthand. Placing the rabbit on his back, they ventured to the feared spot where the menacing sound was first heard. Upon inspection, the reality of the situation unfolded. The lone coconut lay inanimate on a crushed leaf, a simple explanation to a grand tale of fear that had spiraled out of control.

The lion calmly explained the true scenario to the assembled animals, debunking the apocalyptic rumor that had swept through the forest. With a mixture of relief and embarrassment, the animals disbanded, retreating to their peaceful lives.

Lessons:

This tale is reminiscent of how easily misinformation and fear can ripple through communities, even in our modern, well-connected world. One misunderstood event or a misinterpreted message can trigger a cascade of panic and confusion. It's essential to seek truth, to be curious, and to question the waves of information, especially in an era where rumors can travel at the speed of a click. As we navigate through the forests of our lives, may we strive to embody the wisdom and courage of the lion, challenging the status quo, debunking falsehoods, and calming the waves of unwarranted fears. Through this, we foster a society where understanding bridges gaps and truth prevails over fear.

18
Buzz of Enlightenment

Once upon a time, in a little village by a serene lake, lived an old sage and his earnest student named Brittle Cream. One fine morning, they decided to take a walk by the marshy banks of the lake. The tranquility of the scene was briefly interrupted when a mosquito settled on Brittle Cream's arm. Without a second thought, he swatted it away, ending its buzz. "That's the end of its journey," he said, somewhat proudly. "Once buzzing and now silenced forever."

The sage, with a twinkle in his eye, responded, "Every ending marks a new beginning, my friend. Life's essence is its ever-changing nature. Even in the quietest moments, transformation is underway." Just as he finished his words, a mosquito decided to take a chance on the sage's neck. With a swift movement, the sage too, shooed it away into silence. They continued their walk, the ripples in the water seemed to echo the sage's words.

Lessons:

The playful banter with Brittle Cream served as a gentle reminder that change is the only constant thing in life. Whether it's a mosquito's short-lived buzz or our everyday challenges, everything has its time. The sage, with his simple action, demonstrated that life is a cycle of endless beginnings and endings. And it's our response to these small events that shape the larger journey.

In the hustle of modern life, this tale advises us to embrace the transient nature of everything around us. In the face of change, patience isn't about waiting but understanding the rhythm of life. Like the sage, a mindful approach to the small annoyances or big challenges we face paves the way for a balanced existence. The patience in acknowledging a mosquito's buzz, the courage in facing the day's challenges, and the acceptance of life's transient nature, collectively sew the fabric of a peaceful life.

Every interaction, big or small, carries within it a spark of enlightenment, waiting to be discovered. So, as we tread the path of daily life, mirroring the sage's humble wisdom in our actions could be the key to a harmonious existence. Amidst the cacophony of modern life, the age-old tale encourages us to pause, reflect, and navigate the waves of change with a heart full of understanding and a mind imbued with patience.

19

The Vanity Pool

Once upon a time, in a peaceful land where the calm rivers Ganges and Jumna melded, two fish had a chance encounter. They were both mesmerized by each other's appearances.

"I must say, you are quite the sight," complimented the Ganges fish.

"Thank you! You're a looker too," responded the Jumna fish, "though, I've heard that we Jumna fish carry a unique charm." The Ganges fish gasped, "Oh, but it's universally acknowledged that we Ganges fish are the epitome of beauty!"

"No way!" retorted the Jumna fish. "We are the more elegant. Just look at my finesse."

Their banter escalated, with neither willing to back down. They both believed that their river housed the more exquisite fish. They decided to consult an old tortoise, who was soaking up the sun on a nearby rock, hoping he'd settle the dispute.

"Wise tortoise, could you please tell us who among us is more beautiful?" they inquired.

The tortoise examined both fish carefully. Then, with a twinkle in his eye, he said, "Well, you both are fine specimens. However, if we're talking about real beauty, it's all about a stout body, a long neck, a set of sturdy legs, tiny round eyes, and skin that tells tales of time well spent. So, I believe I am the fairest of them all."

The fish was exasperated. "Oh, you are of no help," they sighed. Realizing the fruitlessness of their argument, they parted ways, swimming back to their sides of the riverbank.

Lesson:

The amusing escapade of the fish and the tortoise jolts us gently towards the complexities of vanity and competition. In their brief yet telling encounter, the fish were so immersed in proving their superiority that they lost sight of the fact that beauty is a subjective quality, one that cannot be adjudicated.

In our modern, bustling world, the rat race often blinds us to the reality that worth cannot be measured by mere comparisons. Social media, for instance, can become a pool of comparison, where likes and comments often dictate our perceived self-worth. The story serves as a reminder to step away from the fruitless chase for validation from external sources.

Furthermore, the old tortoise, with his quirky self-assuredness, hints at a sort of self-contentment that's far removed from societal judgments. In a way, his character invites us to embrace our unique traits and find contentment within ourselves, instead of seeking validation through endless comparisons.

Moreover, the self-aware, somewhat cheeky wisdom of the tortoise reflects how, with age and experience, one can look beyond superficial judgments and find a grounding self-assurance. It's a nudge towards cultivating an inner sense of worth, thereby embracing a life of gratitude and contentment over a never-ending competition that leads nowhere fruitful.

Through the interactions in a faraway land, the tale subtly ushers us into reflecting on our own engagements in the modern world – a gentle reminder that there's more to life when we step away from the vain contest and appreciate the beauty in ourselves and in those around us.

20

The Vast Shore and the Tiny Kingdom

Once upon a breezy morning, a grand sea turtle decided to wander along the coastline. During his stroll, he stumbled upon a forsaken shallow well. Peering into it, he saw a little frog dwelling there. "Hey there, little buddy," greeted the turtle, "It looks like you're stuck here. This well seems too deep for you to hop out."

Stuck? Not at all, thought the frog. "Oh, why would I ever wish to leave? It's splendid down here! I have a choir of crickets serenading me, and a pool to frolic in. I'm the ruler of this tiny kingdom," proclaimed the frog with a hint of pride.

The turtle blinked slowly, taking in the frog's perspective, before he attempted to share his own. "Have you ever heard about the sea? It stretches beyond the horizon, embracing miles upon miles. It houses a myriad of creatures, and offers endless adventures awaiting under each wave," the turtle described, his eyes sparkling at the reminiscence of the vast expanse of water and life.

The frog furrowed his brow, trying to grasp the idea, but it seemed too alien, too unimaginable from his well-bound kingdom. "I can't quite picture what you're painting," admitted the frog.

The turtle glanced at the frog's minuscule realm and understood the frog's bounded view. "I guess it's hard to imagine such vastness from this little space. Well, enjoy ruling your kingdom, Your Majesty," he said, with a soft smile. With a slow, patient gait, the turtle continued his journey toward the boundless embrace of the sea.

Lessons:

This simple encounter paints a picture of how different our perspectives can be, based on our experiences and where we find ourselves in life. The frog is content and even proud of his small well kingdom, not knowing of the vastness beyond his familiar grounds. It's not too far off from how we might find ourselves nestled within our comfort zones, convinced that what we have is the pinnacle of existence.

In a modern-day context, we might find ourselves trapped in the 'wells' of our making - perhaps a routine job, a habitual daily schedule, or even a fixed mindset. It's easy to forget there's a vast 'sea' of experiences and perspectives beyond what we know. Just like the turtle and the frog, engaging with others and their diverse experiences can often be a doorway to broader understanding and richer life experiences.

It's worth noting that stepping out from what's known requires a form of courage and curiosity, which can lead to a more colorful and encompassing view of the world around us. It's a gentle nudge to remain open, to explore beyond the familiar, and to respect the different 'seas' and 'wells' of life others may dwell in. Through these humble exchanges, not only do we grow, but we also pave the way for a more compassionate and understanding society, one conversation at a time.

21

The Boozy Beak Brigade

Once upon a breezy morning by the sparkling Arabian Sea near the bustling city of Mumbai, a pair of crows, Mr. and Mrs. CawCaw, hustled along the coastline in their daily quest for grub. The day shone a little brighter when they stumbled upon an abandoned makeshift altar, the remnants of a recent offering to the mighty sea gods, with bits of rice, meat, milk, and a puddle of strong liquor left on it. Their eyes twinkled as they helped themselves to the delightful finds, especially the liquor that tingled down their throats.

Now, with spirits soaring higher than usual, they made their way to the water's edge, where they noticed seabirds merrily gliding over the waves. Mr. CawCaw nudged Mrs. CawCaw and boasted, "Look at them, showing off their water antics. We could do that too, you know." Mrs. CawCaw, with a slightly slurred squawk, agreed, "Absolutely!" So, chuckling, they wobbled into the water, flapping and splashing around. But before they could realize the folly of their antics, a sharp-toothed shark leaped out and snapped Mrs. CawCaw away.

With heart pounding and wings flapping in horror, Mr. CawCaw barely made it back to the shore. He sat there, numb and heartbroken, mourning the loss of his beautiful wife. "Oh, the cruel sea took my lovely wife away!" he wailed. His loud cries gathered a crowd of fellow crows, who huddled around him to understand the reason for his despair. He narrated the tragic tale, conveniently skipping the part about the liquor-fueled misadventure.

A pang of sympathy resonated among the crow crowd, and one of them, not the brightest feather in the flock, suggested a bizarre idea – to drink the sea dry and rescue Mrs. CawCaw from the menacing waves. And with a collective nod, they all dipped their beaks into the salty abyss, gulping down as much as they could. But the sea, vast and endless, seemed to mock their futile endeavor as they drank until their beaks felt sore, and throats burned with the sting of salt.

Exhausted and beaten, they flopped down on the sandy shore. One of them finally squawked, "It's useless. The sea seems to be laughing at our silly attempt." They all agreed, shifting their focus instead on reminiscing about Mrs. CawCaw's captivating beauty, her grace, and the twinkle in her eyes. However, before their memories could turn into an exaggerated saga, a sudden storm sent a lightning bolt across the sky, scaring the flock away, and leaving Mr. CawCaw with his melancholy by the gloomy shore.

Lessons:

The whole adventure carries with it a basket of life morsels. The frolics of Mr. and Mrs. CawCaw touch upon how brief indulgences can lead us to make unwise decisions. It also shows that under distress, people could venture into outlandish solutions without pondering on their feasibility or the logic behind them.

A swift gulp of impulsivity can often lure us into unforeseen predicaments. Whether it's a reckless financial decision spurred by a sudden influx of money or a hasty response in a heated argument, the results often lead to a bitter taste of regret. It reminds us to maintain a balance, to take a step back and evaluate situations rather than diving headlong into them, much like the impromptu dive of our crow couple into the unknown waters.

Furthermore, the well-intended but ill-thought-out rescue attempt by the crow community rings a bell about today's digital era. How often do we find ourselves, or witness others, diving into the ocean of misinformation in an attempt to remedy situations, only to find out we're making no headway and possibly exacerbating the situation? It's a gentle nudge to assess the depth of the waters (or the credibility of the information) before we plunge in.

This story has a touch of humility and mindfulness and we get to learn how to navigate the waves of life with a little more caution and a lot more reflection.

22
The Humble Sojourner

Once, a curious student of a wise sage named Earthen Sky had an unfortunate incident where he ended up eating some spoiled pork dumplings. The experience left him gravely sick, and the sage took it upon himself to nurse Earthen Sky back to health. After a grueling week, Earthen Sky finally showed signs of recovery.

The sage, seeing an opportunity for a lesson, asked, "You were on the brink, my student. Were you afraid of death?"

"Oh, absolutely," responded Earthen Sky, his face pale from the ordeal.

"Allow me to share a tale that might help you steer away from the jaws of death," the sage began. "Once in a lush, boundless forest lived a crow known among the avian community as 'the shy one.' Unlike his peers, he never took the lead when they soared across the sky; he was always content fluttering near the end. His choice of branch was always a bit secluded from the rest. During feeding times, he patiently waited, pecking at the leftovers only after others had had their fill. He never craved recognition nor did he flaunt his flights. This cautious demeanor, distant from the rush and the showoff, granted him a life of tranquility and longevity, outliving all his feathered companions."

The sage paused, letting the essence of the story marinate in Earthen Sky's recovering mind.

Lessons:
This simple tale underlines a life led with cautiousness and humility, illustrating a path often less trodden in the hustle of modern times. In an age where the race to the top can become the sole focus, the idea of staying a bit on the sidelines, savoring the calm, and extending a patient hand, can indeed unveil a life less chaotic and more rewarding.

The tale of the shy crow is reflective of how a subtle retreat from the clamor for recognition could lead to a life of peace, lesser stress, and perhaps, longevity. Much like the sage's tender care for Earthen Sky, the narrative extends a gentle reminder that in patience and humility, there's much to be discovered and cherished. While our endeavors push us to strive for excellence, a step back, much like the shy crow's flight, could provide a vantage point where life's simple and profound lessons become apparent. This retelling invites a pause, an examination of the pace of life, and a humble acknowledgment of the quiet, less-trodden path that also leads to a fulfilling and longer life.

23

The Shimmering Friend

Once, nestled amidst the lush landscapes of northeastern India, lived a golden mallard, known far and wide for his dazzling feathers that were of genuine gold. Aware of human covetousness, the mallard maintained a safe distance, veiling himself in the thick foliage. Yet, in a quiet corner of this verdant home, lived a widow with her two daughters, humble in means but rich in heart. The mallard observed them from afar, his heart warming up to the innocent girls, who despite their penury, radiated kindness.

One sunlit morning, the mallard soared towards their humble abode, descending upon the roof. Delighted, the girls cried out to their mother, showcasing their avian visitor. The mother, too, was struck by the beauty of the bird. Sensing their hardship, the mallard offered them a single feather, with a promise to return with more to alleviate their want. The mother graciously accepted the feather, which they traded for sustenance and clothing.

Over time, the mallard kept his promise, visiting them with a feather each time, enriching their modest lives. The small home now bustled with contentment, the girls and their mother now wore smiles as warm as the new dresses that adorned them.

But one day, fear gnawed at the mother's peace. "What if the mallard ceases to visit us?" she worried, envisioning a return to the days of want. She shared her worry with her daughters, suggesting a plan to capture the mallard and pluck all his golden feathers. The girls were horrified by the thought, their hearts aching at the thought of causing pain to their benign benefactor.

However, the next visit by the mallard saw the mother's fear overshadow her gratitude. She seized the mallard, plucking away all the golden feathers, leaving the mallard bereft and piteous. Yet, in her haste, she witnessed the golden hue fading away, each plucked feather morphing into ordinary gray, the magic waning with her greed.

Disheartened, the mother lamented the vanished fortune while her daughters wept for the mallard. They tended to the bird with whatever little they had, nursing him back to health with love and patience. The mallard too, recuperated over time, growing back ordinary feathers, bidding farewell to the humble abode but with a promise to visit his compassionate friends. As he fluttered away, his heart carried a melancholy note towards human greed, but also a melodious tune of love, care, and the invaluable lesson of contentment.

Lessons:

This tale of The Shimmering Friend sheds light on some profound virtues, threading the delicate balance between gratitude, contentment, and the sinister shadows of greed. The impoverished family initially welcomes the golden mallard's altruism, finding a soothing respite from their daily struggles. But soon, fear entwined with greed clouds the mother's judgment, leading to a calamitous loss.

In today's modern setting, it's easy to get ensnared in the perpetual want for more, overlooking the basic ethos of gratitude and contentment. Our material pursuits, akin to the mother's anxious desires, often blind us to the beauty and simplicity of what we already have. On a broader spectrum, the narrative speaks volumes about human interaction with nature, reflecting on our avaricious tendencies that often lead to environmental degradation, much like the fading gold of the mallard's plumes.

However, hope is symbolized by the compassionate daughters who prioritize love and care over transient material gain, embodying the essence of kindness and patience. This timeless lesson encourages adults to look beyond mere materialistic pursuits, nurturing a heart full of gratitude, patience, and love. By embodying these virtues, we can foster a more harmonious existence, resonating with the simple yet profound humaneness showcased by the daughters.

24

The Dance of Fortune

Once, in a distant land, there lived a wise sage who had a curious student named Liquid Cartwheels. Over time, Liquid Cartwheels moved on and took a lucrative position as a consultant to a king in a neighboring realm. However, misfortune struck when a rebellion overthrew the king, causing Liquid Cartwheels to lose his esteemed position. Fleeing the chaos, he returned to his master, bewildered and defeated.

"Why has fate turned so bitter? Just a while ago, I basked in comfort and wealth, now I stand before you, a pauper," lamented Liquid Cartwheels.

His master, peering into the horizon, responded, "Have you observed a gibbon navigating through trees? In a tree with smooth branches, the gibbon dances through with elegance, effortlessly. However, when it encounters a thorny tree, its movement becomes cautious, almost awkward as it navigates through the prickly hurdles. You, my dear Liquid Cartwheels, find yourself amidst thorns now. Tread carefully, and in time, you may find your smooth branches again."

Lessons:

Sometimes, we find ourselves cruising effortlessly, much like the gibbon amid smooth branches. Then, without warning, we are amidst thorns. Our dance, once fluid, now demands a meticulous, almost clumsy maneuver through challenges.

It's through such contrasts, we learn to value patience and a cautious stride. The situation of Liquid Cartwheels resembles that of many who face abrupt changes in life's circumstances, say losing a job or experiencing unforeseen mishaps. Such episodes might appear as setbacks but are merely part of life's undulating journey. The sage's counsel about moving cautiously through the thorny patches is a metaphor for navigating life's ups and downs. It also subtly instills a sense of hope; the idea that good times are akin to the smooth-branched tree, always within reach if one navigates the challenges with patience and care.

In modern times, where change is the only constant, this story resonates profoundly. It urges us to embrace patience, acknowledge the transient nature of adversity, and continue our dance amidst both smooth and thorny paths, in hopes of better times ahead. Through the sage's wisdom, we're reminded to retain our grace and hope, irrespective of the tree we find ourselves in. And just like Liquid Cartwheels, we too might find our smooth branches again, as long as we continue navigating with diligence and hope.

25

A Clever Encounter

Once upon a time in the outskirts of the bustling city of Varanasi, lived a young partridge amidst the expansive cultivated fields. His daily routine was quite straightforward— hopping around on the plowed mounds, pecking at the delicious seeds unearthed by the diligent farmers. The soft mounds hardened under the intense gaze of the Indian sun as the day progressed.

This young partridge had grown with the wisdom of his father, who showed him the ropes of finding the finest seeds while being cautious. However, on one particularly hot day, the routine felt mundane to the young bird. He recalled whispers of a refreshing shelter at the forest's fringe, where the sun's harsh rays were softened by the canopy and the ground was rich with delightful seeds. Unable to resist the allure, he soared towards this promising sanctuary.

On reaching, the partridge reveled in the cool ambiance and the abundant feast at his disposal. Unbeknownst to him, a hawk sat perched high upon a barren branch, keeping a keen eye on the happenings below. As the partridge indulged, the hawk seized the moment, soared higher, then descended silently with a swoop, clutching the partridge within his powerful talons, envisioning a hearty meal atop his favored perch.

Realizing the peril he was in, the partridge exclaimed loudly, hoping to pierce through the hawk's intent, "Oh, what folly has befallen me! I shouldn't have strayed from my familiar abode. This grave error wouldn't have occurred on the fields I call home."

His words were met with a smug chuckle from the hawk, prompting him to continue, "Indeed, had I been on my turf, facing you wouldn't have been a dread."

Amused, the hawk queried, "And where might this grand battlefield be, where a partridge can stand against a hawk?"

"In the open plowed field where I have mastered the art of survival," responded the partridge, poised in his belief.

Mocking the partridge's audacity, the hawk retorted, "This spectacle I have to witness! Let's adjourn to your field for this epic duel."

The hawk then loosened his grip, setting the partridge free who hastily winged his way to his familiar field. He landed atop a colossal, rock-hard mound of dirt, with a protective ledge behind. As the hawk circled above, the partridge beckoned, "I am ready, Mr. Hawk."

With a fierce dive, the hawk plunged towards the partridge who stood unflinching, only to dart back under the ledge at the last moment. The hawk collided with the rigid mound, knocking him unconscious.

Standing atop the mound, the partridge mused, "Father's words ring true: there's safety in familiar grounds."

Lessons:

Drawing from this story, there's an air of familiarity and comfort that our routine and known surroundings provide. This young partridge, in his moment of exploration, stepped into the unknown, which unfortunately led him into peril. However, the clever use of his familiar terrain saved him from the looming danger.

In a rapidly evolving world where venturing into the unknown is often celebrated, it's essential to not disregard the value of the known. Each sphere, the known and the unknown, has its significance. While the known offers a sense of safety and mastery, the unknown propels growth through challenges.

It's an art to balance the intrigue of the unknown with the comfort of the known. Our careers, relationships, and personal endeavors are fields where such balance could be sought. Whether it's a career switch, embracing new relationships, or adopting novel ideologies, a gentle balance could act as a compass.

Moreover, the arrogance of the hawk and the tactical cleverness of the partridge depict that no matter how powerful or knowledgeable one believes they are, there's always room for unexpected outcomes. It's a reminder to stay humble, acknowledge our roots, and utilize our core strengths, especially when navigating through life's myriad challenges.

26

The Chain of Distraction

Once upon a time, under the comforting shade of towering pine, a wise sage was about to drift into an afternoon slumber when his young disciple, Iron Willow, rushed towards him, panting and distraught. He gasped, "Master, I was meant to watch over my younger brother, but a pretty girl caught my eye. Meanwhile, my brother climbed a tree, fell, and now his arm is broken. I fear the wrath of my mother when I return home."

Iron Willow's heart raced as the sage calmly turned his gaze upon him and began to speak. "Iron Willow, a hunter was wandering through the king's lush chestnut grove with his trusted bow by his side. As he strolled, he looked up and saw a cicada nestled on a branch, savoring the sap. Just above, a praying mantis was inching closer to the cicada, and above them both, a magpie perched, eyeing the mantis eagerly. Suddenly, in a swift wave of action, the mantis snatched the cicada, the magpie swooped down grabbing the mantis, and at that moment, the hunter's arrow found its mark on the magpie.

All three — the cicada, the praying mantis, and the magpie — were engrossed in what was directly in front of them, oblivious to the greater danger lurking. Likewise, you were entranced by the girl and overlooked your responsibility towards your brother. Now, the outcome of that distraction awaits you."

Lessons:

The tale highlights the ripple of consequences that arise from a single moment of distraction. It's an echo of modern times where distractions are plentiful. In a world buzzing with constant notifications, social media alerts, and endless streams of digital enticements, it's easy to lose sight of our primary duties. Whether it's overseeing a project at work, nurturing relationships, or ensuring the safety and well-being of loved ones, a fleeting moment of inattention can lead to a cascade of unforeseen events.

Being present and mindful in our actions is a lesson wrapped within this tale, a reminder of the delicate balance between our desires and our responsibilities. It's about understanding that our actions, or the lack thereof, have consequences that often extend beyond our immediate sphere, impacting others in ways we might not have anticipated.

By tuning into the present, we become more adept at navigating through life's responsibilities with a sense of awareness and attentiveness, akin to a sage under a calm shade, aware and at peace amidst the unpredictable whirl of life.

27

Monkey Business in the Royal Garden

Once, in the lush royal garden of Varanasi, a lively group of monkeys thrived, enjoying an endless supply of food and absolute safety. The sole caretaker of this garden was a humble gardener, who, one day, decided to attend a week-long festival in the city. However, he had just planted some young saplings which needed watering in four days. An idea popped into his mind — why not entrust this simple task to the monkeys? They seemed smart enough to handle it.

He approached the monkey leader, highlighted how fortunate they were to reside in such a bountiful garden, and requested them to water the young trees while he was away. The leader agreed enthusiastically. The gardener, feeling reassured, handed them some watering pots and set off to enjoy the festival.

Four days later, as decided, the monkey leader gathered his troop, distributed the watering pots, and instructed them to water the trees. Chaos ensued as monkeys scampered around, tossing water everywhere, with most of it splashing on the leaves and barely any reaching the soil. The leader realized the error but wasn't sure about the amount of water each tree needed. So, he devised a plan - to uproot each tree, check the length of its roots, and water them accordingly; more water for longer roots, less for shorter ones.

The troop hailed the leader for his 'brilliant' idea and went about uprooting every single sapling. The result was predictably catastrophic. Even though they meticulously followed the new watering 'protocol', the young trees couldn't withstand the shock of being uprooted and began to wither away almost instantly.

Meanwhile, two of the king's advisors happened to stroll through the garden and witnessed the bizarre scene. Intrigued, they inquired a monkey about their actions, who proudly narrated the entire episode. One advisor remarked to the other, "Here we see how well-intentioned actions, when executed without understanding or wisdom, lead to disaster." The other nodded, adding, "Indeed. And it's bewildering to think that the gardener believed monkeys could handle such a task."

Lessons:

Discussing this amusing yet insightful incident, unravels the importance of assigning tasks to capable hands, understanding the nuances of responsibility before diving headlong into it, and the calamities that could follow otherwise. It brings light to modern workplaces or even in our daily chores, where sometimes tasks are handed over without much thought on the suitability or capability of the individual. Similarly, it reflects upon the need to respect and understand the nature and requirements of the tasks we undertake. If we dive into actions without fully grasping the essence or the demands of the task, the results might not only be ineffective but could potentially cause harm or setback to the intended cause.

In a world bustling with eagerness to get things done quickly, pausing to understand, think, and then act could sometimes save a lot of effort and prevent unintended negative consequences.

The Joyful Swim

Once, a sage named Grey Feather and his student, Little Sparrow found themselves in a quaint village after a long stroll through a dense woodland. They decided to stop by a modest street vendor and purchased two bowls of warm, comforting soup to nourish themselves. As they sat on a weathered bench, savoring the simple meal, Little Sparrow turned to his teacher with a curious glint in his eyes. He asked, "Master, what makes a ruler truly great, so his people can live in joy and contentment?"

Grey Feather, with a gentle smile, began to narrate an old tale from days of yore. "Many moons ago, the venerable Green Emperor was on a voyage across his vast kingdom, accompanied by his loyal ministers. During their travels, they chanced upon an old fisherman by a calm lake. This humble man had a peculiar way of fishing – he used a red silk line that carried no hook. Yet, around this hookless line frolicked a school of joyful fish, swimming without fear or restraint. The scene struck a chord with the Emperor, and he declared to his ministers, 'Let this wise fisherman be my chief minister and oversee my realms.' He knew a compassionate heart could guide without instilling fear. Following this, the Green Emperor retreated to a peaceful life amid the towering peaks."

Lessons:

The tale encapsulates the essence of gentle leadership, showcasing how one doesn't need to be severe or controlling to govern. The Green Emperor recognized that a sense of tranquility and care emanated from the humble fisherman, which resonated with the free-spirited fish, creating an environment of trust and happiness. Drawing inspiration from the past, modern leaders too can foster a culture of understanding and empathy, guiding with a soft hand yet firm resolve, ensuring both the happiness of the people and the progress of society.

In today's fast-paced world, the narrative reminds us to reflect upon our actions, whether as leaders in our own right or as individuals interacting with others. It beckons us to embody patience, understanding, and a calm demeanor as we navigate the tumultuous waters of modern existence, impacting the world one gentle ripple at a time.

29

Sweet Lies and Sour Reality

Once upon a time near the bustling city of Varanasi, there existed a lush grove of rose apple trees. The time of harvest had dawned upon the grove, and a crow found itself nestled on a branch, feasting on the sweet offerings of the tree. The jackal, known for its crafty ways, roamed the grove with hunger dancing in its eyes. It soon spotted the crow, which was seated on a high perch, indulging in the fruit that the jackal so dearly desired but couldn't reach.

An idea sparked in the mind of the jackal, knowing the crow's tendency toward vanity. "Ah, if I charm this bird with sweet words, perhaps I could share in this sweet feast," thought the jackal.

With a dramatic flair, the jackal began, "Oh, what divine melody graces my ears from yonder tree? Surely, it must be the symphony of the most exquisite songbird. Ah, now my eyes bear witness to this spectacle! A being with feathers more splendid than a peacock, embodying grace and charm. Verily, this must be a noble creature, the epitome of avian elegance!" The crow, swayed by this orchestration of flattery, puffed its chest in pride.

Responding to the jackal's deceitful admiration, the crow said, "Ah, it's a mark of noble lineage to acknowledge one of its kind. You, dear friend, possess the majestic grace of a young, fierce tiger. Allow me to share this heavenly bounty with you." And with a vigorous shake of its branch, the crow showered the jackal with a rain of rose apples, thus fulfilling the jackal's cunning desire.

In a nearby tree, an owl had been a silent witness to this exchange of superficial pleasantries. It shook its head in disdain and commented, "Such scavengers, reveling in falsehood, living off the remnants of the world, they represent the dire straits of sincerity in this world." Feeling a bitter taste amidst the sweet ambiance of the grove, the owl took flight to seek a quieter, more honest part of the forest.

Lessons:

The narrative sheds light on the ease with which flattery can blind one to reality, and how superficial praises can lead to undeserved rewards. In today's world, where social validation is often sought and given easily, the tale calls upon individuals to exercise discernment. It speaks to the integrity of character, urging one to see beyond superficial praises and to engage in authentic interactions.

The exchange between the crow and the jackal also highlights the transient nature of deceptive gains. While the jackal may have satisfied its immediate hunger, the absence of an honest interaction ensures the lack of a meaningful connection or a lasting reward. As for the crow, its vanity led to the loss of its prized possession to deceit.

In today's increasingly virtual world, the allure of hollow admiration can often eclipse the essence of sincere connections. The story is a gentle reminder to uphold sincerity over fleeting validations and to nurture genuine interactions that enrich our lives in a profound manner.

30

A Quick Peek

Once, not too long ago, in a little wooden cabin nestled amidst a lush forest, an old sage and his student named Sweet Boulder sat silently, sipping their warm cups of tea. The calm ambiance was briefly interrupted when Sweet Boulder, peering through a small crack in the wall, caught a glimpse of a deer darting through the woods. "Master, through this crack, I think I saw a deer gallop past. But it was gone in a flash!" he exclaimed.

The sage, with a serene smile, responded, "Ah, the moment you saw the deer fleet by is much like how our lives rush past. Every moment is precious."

Lessons:

In this modest interaction, the old sage and Sweet Boulder remind us of life's swift pace. Often, we get lost in our routine, forgetting to pause and savor the simple joys around us. This tale tells us to appreciate the fleeting moments, much like that fleeting glimpse of the deer.

Today, it's easy to overlook the beauty and spontaneous joy in small, fleeting experiences. Being anchored at the moment, much like Sweet Boulder was when he saw the deer, invites us to embrace the transient nature of life with a gracious heart.

31

Granny's Gentle Giant

Once upon a time, in a humble village nestled a little way outside the bustling city of Varanasi, resided a kind-hearted widow. Many years ago, her brother had aided a wealthy merchant in the city, who to express his gratitude, bestowed unique gifts upon the entire family. The gift that fell into the widow's lap was a baby elephant. The widow was overjoyed and nurtured the elephant like her own, feeding it rice and porridge, tirelessly laboring to keep up with the creature's growing appetite as it blossomed into adulthood.

The exceptionally dark elephant earned the name "Granny's Blackie" by the villagers. He seamlessly integrated into the village community, forming a special bond with the children who found a playful companion in him. They would scamper around with Blackie by the river, giggle as he swung them gently with his trunk, and shriek with joy when he splashed river water over them.

One fine morning, as they played by the river, Blackie implored the widow to join them. Despite her yearning to enjoy the tranquil river, the widow had to decline, encumbered by her daily chores. It dawned upon Blackie the strenuous life the widow led to sustain them both, while he frolicked under the sun. He was struck by a thought, "It's about time I lightened Granny's burden."

The subsequent day brought a stroke of fate. A caravan owner, anxious to transport five hundred carts laden with merchandise to Varanasi, found himself at a river's bend. His oxen were struggling, failing to haul the carts over the rugged riverbed, even at its shallowest. His eyes met Blackie's sturdy frame, playing by the river with the children. Upon inquiring, he learned about the widow and struck a deal: two coins for every cart Blackie could haul across the river.

Eager to ease the widow's toil, Blackie set to work, pulling one cart after another. It was demanding yet his robust form persevered, drawing all five hundred carts across. But when the caravan owner handed over a sack containing only five hundred coins, Blackie's heart sank. He knew he was shortchanged. He promptly laid himself down, blocking the caravan's passage. The owner, realizing his deceit was caught, rectified his mistake by adding the rightful five hundred coins.

Blackie, content, raced back to the village, the kids cheering alongside. The widow, upon seeing Blackie's exhausted state, was initially taken aback but soon the entire tale unfolded. Overwhelmed with pride, she along with the children, led Blackie to the river, cleaning the tired but triumphant gentle giant. From then on, occasional jobs for Blackie ensured a comfortable living for him and the widow, who spent her remaining days in solace and content.

Lessons:

This simple tale reflects how a conscious shift in recognizing and addressing not just one's needs, but that of others too, can lead to a ripple effect of positive outcomes. Just like Blackie, stepping out of one's comfort zone and extending a hand can not only bring relief to others but also foster a sense of community and shared joy. It encourages the importance of fairness, gratitude, and the value of hard work, relevant notions in today's fast-paced world, where sometimes, the essence of community and rightful earning takes a backseat. Through simple acts of awareness and kindness, one can significantly elevate not just their own life but others as well, showcasing that every effort counts, no matter how colossal or minute.

32

The Simple Wisdom of the Wild

Once upon a time, in a quiet village, lived a wise old sage and his curious pupil named Marble Toe. On one warm summer evening, they found themselves sitting under the comforting shade of a large tree, the air around them filled with the quiet hum of nature. Marble Toe, always inquisitive, broke the silence with a thought that had been nesting in his mind.

"You know, I've always heard that to maintain order among people, it's essential to have rules, a fair bit of regulation, and punishments for those who step out of line," said Marble Toe, looking to the sage for an insight.

The sage, with a gentle smile, nodded and glanced at the little creatures around them. "That's a common thought, indeed. However, have you ever considered how the creatures of the wild manage? Take a mouse, for instance. If you try to confine it with rules, it'll find its way into a hole, escaping any barriers you set. Or consider a bird, if you attempt to regulate its path, it'll simply soar higher into the sky. And ah, the monkey, if you think of punishing it, you'd have to first endeavor to catch it, a feat easier said than done. Humans aren't too different, my dear Marble Toe. The more rules you set, the more some will yearn to break free."

Marble Toe absorbed the sage's words, letting the gentle wisdom wash over him. The sage continued, "Instead of a labyrinth of rules if we observe and learn from the simple, harmonious ways of nature, we'd realize the beauty of fewer rules. In simplicity and understanding, you'll find that there's seldom a need for regulations or punishments."

Lessons:
As Marble Toe pondered on the sage's words, he realized the profound simplicity of the sage's teaching. In our modern world, where life often feels entangled in numerous rules and

expectations, there's a gentle invitation to look towards simplicity. It pokes us to consider whether the complex web of rules we surround ourselves with, serves us or entangles us further.

The story subtly encourages us to reflect on our surroundings, our interactions with others, and the systems we abide by. It beckons a consideration, of whether a simpler approach, akin to the natural order of things, might foster a more harmonious, understanding, and less punitive existence. Through a delicate narrative, adults are guided to reflect on the essence of simplicity and understanding in fostering a more harmonious life, much like the serene coexistence observed in the wilderness.

The Clever Coin-Carrying Mouse and the Stone-hearted Stonecutter

Once upon a time, not too far from the bustling city of Varanasi, there existed a forgotten village, housing nothing but an empty, old residence that became home to a witty Mother Mouse. Unbeknownst to many, the house concealed a treasure of gold coins left by a bygone merchant. The mouse discovered this bounty but found no use for it until she noticed a lone stonecutter working tirelessly at a nearby quarry. His gentle demeanor touched the mouse's heart. One fine morning, she decided to share her fortune with him.

With a golden coin clutched in her mouth, she approached the stonecutter who was both amazed and humbled by her gesture. Their exchange became a daily spectacle, a coin for a chunk of meat. However, their quaint routine was disrupted when a cat discovered Mother Mouse, tempted by a quick, easy meal. The clever mouse offered a deal, daily meat in return for her life. The agreement was sealed, but soon, more cats came into the picture, leaving almost nothing for the mouse as she divided the meat among them.

Worried, the stonecutter inquired about the Mother Mouse's deteriorating health. Once informed, he hatched a brilliant plan. He crafted a transparent crystal sanctuary for the mouse to protect her from the prowling cats while tricking them into believing she had magical powers. This clever deception scared the cats away, never to return.

Thankful, Mother Mouse revealed the treasure to the stonecutter. With pockets full and heart's content, they moved into a cozy abode where laughter, companionship, and comfort adorned the rest of their days.

Lessons:

This simple yet thought-evoking tale nudges us towards a realm of understanding that often, the act of sharing and caring springs from the most unexpected quarters, painting the essence of compassion and gratitude in pure, untouched strokes. Our stonecutter didn't hesitate to share his meal, while our witty mouse didn't think twice before offering her treasure, fostering a bond that bloomed with trust and respect over time.

In today's world, it's not the possession but the intention that counts. The narrative subtly prompts us to overlook the common pursuit of materialistic gains and cherish the unnoticed, humble gestures that resonate with genuine concern and empathy. Moreover, it's about facing adversities with a bit of wit and lots of courage, never hesitating to seek or offer help when in need, and enriching our lives with unforeseen friendships and heartwarming experiences.

Through the playful interaction between a modest stonecutter and a clever mouse, we're reminded of the endless possibilities that simple acts of kindness and a little ingenuity can unfold, painting our mundane routines with strokes of unexpected joy and contentment.

34

The Humble Wanderer

Once, in a quiet village, a wise old man and his students were enjoying a calm morning beside a slow-moving river. They were leisurely fishing, though the fish seemed uninterested in their bait. Out of nowhere, a grand carriage adorned with gold accents made its way toward them. It was carrying one of the king's top officials. The official, with a respectful bow, approached the old man, "Dear sage, the king admires your wisdom greatly and wishes for you to be his chief advisor at the court."

The old man, not diverting his attention from the fishing pole, responded, "I've heard the king possesses the shell of a sacred tortoise, a creature a thousand years old. Is that true?"

"Yes," the official nodded, "It's one of the treasured possessions of the kingdom."

"Tell me," the old man asked, "Do you think that tortoise would have preferred to be an honored artifact beside the king or to be alive, exploring the desert in search of greens?"

The official thought for a moment before replying, "I believe it would have preferred to be alive."

"Me too," said the old man, "I'd rather be a tortoise, free to wander the desert."

The official, understanding the metaphor, climbed back into his carriage and returned to the palace, carrying the old man's wise words with him.

Lessons:

The simplicity of the old man's desires highlights a profound insight. Many chase after titles, prestige, or societal validation, losing sight of the simple joys life has to offer. It's a gentle reminder in our fast-paced world where ambition often overrules contentment. It's easy to get caught up in the race for recognition or wealth, yet this story reminds us to consider what truly matters - the freedom to live authentically, the tranquility found in nature, and the value of a less complicated existence.

Drawing a parallel, this narrative encourages adults to re-evaluate what happiness means to them. It's not always about climbing the societal ladder but finding contentment in the simple, unadorned corners of life. Our modern world, with its relentless emphasis on more - more success, more wealth, more followers - can often lead us away from the essence of a fulfilling life. Like the wise old man who found joy in the simplicity of a leisurely day by the river, maybe it's a nudge for us to find our own 'slow-moving river' amidst the chaos, and to be content with the simple, yet profound joy it brings.

35

Crafty Capers in Crocodile Cove

Once, in a lush jungle south of Varanasi, lived a clever little monkey. He resided by a serene river, which had a fanciful island in the middle, adorned with the juiciest fruit trees one could find. Every day, the monkey would leap onto a solitary rock mid-river, then onto the island to feast on sweet fruits and return home by evening.

Nearby, a pair of crocodiles dwelt in the same stretch of river. The female crocodile, enamored by the monkey's plump physique, fancied having him for dinner. She convinced her partner to catch the monkey for her, and although hesitant, he agreed.

The male crocodile devised a simple plan. He would disguise himself as the rock the monkey leaps onto, and when the monkey jumped onto him, it would be dinner time. He chose the dim lighting of the evening for his ploy, positioning his massive head on top of the rock.

As dusk approached, the monkey, with a belly full of fruits, decided to head home. As he was about to leap, he noticed the rock seemed higher than usual. Sensing something amiss, he called out, "Mr. Rock, oh, Mr. Rock, how are you tonight?" There was no response. He called out again, "Mr. Rock, my friend, why don't you answer me tonight?"

Thinking that the rock usually responds, the crocodile played along, "Hello my fine monkey friend, how are you this lovely evening?"

"I'm just fine," retorted the monkey, "but you certainly are not a rock. Who are you and what do you want?"

The crocodile came clean, "I am a crocodile, and my wife desires to have you for dinner."

Quick-wittedly, the monkey said, "Well, it seems like I have no choice but to oblige. Open your mouth wide and I'll jump right in." Knowing crocodiles close their eyes when they open their mouths, the monkey leaped onto the crocodile's head instead, bounded to the river bank, and scampered away to safety.

Looking back at the disoriented crocodile, the monkey cheekily said, "Your wife will have to find a different meal tonight." The crocodile returned home with a heavy heart, dreading to tell his mate of his failed promise.

Lessons:

This tale, wrapped in humor and wit, unveils a message of quick thinking and adaptability. The monkey, with his astute observation and sharp reflexes, navigates a perilous situation, teaching a valuable lesson in handling unexpected challenges. In a modern world filled with unforeseen hurdles, adapting quickly often becomes the key to turning peril into triumph. Additionally, the story sheds light on the idea of not succumbing to pressure or dangerous enticements, an ever-pertinent lesson in today's age where myriad distractions abound.

Just as the monkey didn't fall for the crocodile's trick, individuals too can exercise discernment and quick thinking in precarious situations, whether it's in navigating tricky social scenarios or making split-second decisions in a traffic jam. The narrative urges one to remain observant, think on their feet, and not fall for deceptive allure, ensuring a safe passage through the metaphorical rivers of modern life.

36

The Pea Pursuit

Once upon a time, in the royal city of Varanasi, there was a mischievous monkey who loved lingering around the royal stables, high up on a tree, overseeing the feeding trough of the king's beloved horses. One sunny morning, the trough was brimming with steamed peas, a delicacy the monkey adored. Without a second thought, the monkey swung down, filled his mouth and hands with the delicious green orbs, and scurried back up to enjoy his feast.

As he nibbled on his loot with glee, a single pea slipped from his grasp and tumbled down to the ground. Anxiety gripped the monkey. He hastily scrambled down the tree, dropping his precious hoard of peas one by one. He scoured the ground for the lost pea but to no avail. Meanwhile, the horses munched away on the peas in the trough and the scattered ones on the ground. By the time the monkey gave up, there wasn't a single pea left. Crestfallen, he climbed back to his perch, only to be greeted by the laughter of the stable hands who had been watching the scene unfold.

At that moment, the king and his advisor approached the stables to check on the horses and caught the last act of the monkey's misadventure. The king turned to his advisor, curious about his take on the situation. The advisor, weighing his words carefully, remarked, "Your Majesty, what unfolded here is not uncommon. Many times, individuals, be they common folk or kings, lose sight of the bigger picture in the scramble for trivial gains. The attempt to retrieve a single pea led to the loss of many, much like how one might squander a fortune over a trifling matter or even a king might jeopardize his realm over minor disputes."

The king absorbed the advisor's reflection, recognizing the wisdom in acknowledging one's losses, however small, and moving forward rather than dwelling on them or letting them multiply.

Lessons:

These days, such situations are not hard to find. In the chase for what often appears immediately desirable or momentarily upsetting, we might lose sight of what holds real value. It's a delicate balance to maintain, learning when to let go of a single 'pea' to preserve the rest. Whether it's in our personal relationships, professional endeavors, or the broader societal dynamics, understanding the essence of what truly matters, being patient, and exercising discernment could steer us away from needless losses and towards a path of meaningful pursuits.

37

A Glimpse of Gold and Feathers

Once upon a time, in a quiet village, lived an old sage and his student named Marble Eggshell. One fine morning, while they were on their regular walk, they saw a magnificent golden coach rushing past them. The coach, adorned with precious gems, was pulled by two strong, jet-black horses. It was carrying the king's chief minister, who looked radiant in his elegant attire.

Marble Eggshell looked at the coach with wide eyes and said, "Oh, how marvelous it must be to have such wealth and to travel in such grand style rather than tread on this dusty road!"

The sage, smiling gently, responded, "Ah, but wealth and grandeur aren't suited for everyone, just like they aren't for the white peacock."

Seeing the puzzled look on his student's face, the sage shared a story: "Once, in a remote part of the forest, a hunter in the king's service discovered a white peacock, its feathers shimmering with a heavenly glow. The hunter was mesmerized and decided to capture the peacock for the king. After many attempts, he finally succeeded and presented the bird to the king, who was in awe of its beauty. The king decided to honor the peacock with a grand banquet.

During the banquet, the royal musicians played melodious tunes, but the loud music scared the delicate bird. The court dancers swirled gracefully, but their rapid movements unnerved the peacock. When the royal chefs brought out dishes laden with rich meats, the scent made the peacock nauseous. Overwhelmed by the surge of unfamiliar sights, sounds, and smells, the delicate bird couldn't bear the burden of royal attention. It trembled and, with a final shudder, fell lifeless."

Concluding his narrative, the sage glanced at his student and remarked, "Similar to the white peacock, some of us are not built for a life laden with riches. A simpler, quieter path offers its own kind of richness."

Marble Eggshell nodded, absorbing the deeper meaning of the sage's words as they continued their walk.

Lessons:

This tale reflects a profound truth: the external allure of wealth and status can often be deceiving. In our contemporary hustle for material success, it's easy to overlook the inherent value of simplicity and the peace that accompanies a life devoid of relentless worldly pursuits. Not everyone finds comfort in a life adorned with riches; some find it in the serenity of simplicity, in the chirping of birds rather than the jingle of gold.

Moreover, this story quietly shows us the importance for us to recognize and honor our innate nature, instead of getting swept away in society's opulent desires. Like the sage and Marble Eggshell, we all have a path that feels right and a pace that feels natural. And in recognizing and respecting that, we find our own version of richness, irrespective of society's golden standards.

Lastly, just as the white peacock, the sage, and his student teach us the significance of staying true to one's essence amidst a world constantly bustling with the noise of more. Through their simple day-to-day existence, they invite us to explore a life that resonates with our true selves, thereby nurturing a kind of wealth that's more enduring and personally fulfilling.

The Sly Arbitrator

Once upon a time, nestled beside a winding river that merged into the mighty Ganges, lived a pair of playful otters. Not too far from their riverbank, in a modest den, dwelled two jackals who made their living scavenging along the river's shores.

On a sun-drenched morning, as one of the otters was prancing around in the river, he stumbled upon a hefty rohita fish. The fish was stout and attempted to swim away, pulling the otter along. He yelped for his companion, who swiftly came to his aid. With a tag-team effort, they were able to pull the fish ashore.

Panting and weary, they sprawled beside their catch, admiring its size.

As they regained their breath, a discussion sparked between them on how to split the fish fairly. Their talk escalated into a squabble and it seemed a resolution was far from sight.

During this melee, a jackal from the nearby den strolled along, spotting the otters and their catch. The otters, seeing an opportunity for a fair division, called out to the jackal, "Kind Jackal, could you assist us in dividing this catch? We can't seem to agree."

The jackal strutted over, puffed up with a sense of importance. "Certainly," he declared, "I have resolved many such disputes with grace." Upon understanding the circumstances, he examined the fish meticulously. Suddenly, he instructed one otter to take the head and the other the tail. The otters, although puzzled, complied, awaiting the next move.

With a swift action, the jackal claimed the bulky middle part, announcing it as his fee for the service, and dashed off leaving the otters holding the mere remnants of their catch.

The otter with the tail sighed, dropping it to the ground, "Had we not been clouded by greed, we'd be feasting right now."

His friend, dropping his head, nodded in agreement, "A lesson hard learned."

In the den, the jackal shared his spoils with his mate, reveling in the day's unforeseen fortune.

Lessons:

In this tale, the otters' inability to compromise led them to seek external arbitration, which resulted in the loss of their cherished catch. It reminds adults of the necessity to find common ground, especially in an age where disagreements can escalate rapidly, often leading to undesirable outcomes.

In today's complex society, disputes are common, whether in personal relationships, within communities, or on a global stage. The need for effective communication and compromise is essential to foster a culture of understanding and mutual respect. Like the otters, sometimes our unwillingness to compromise, driven by individual desires or greed, can lead to unforeseen consequences. The external arbitrator, represented by the jackal, is sometimes the system or individuals who might take advantage of such situations for personal gain.

The narrative also sheds light on the essence of greed and the importance of learning life lessons, albeit the hard way. It prompts reflection on how our actions, driven by self-interest, may lead to unfavorable outcomes, and how a shift towards a more cooperative and less self-centered approach can lead to better, mutually beneficial resolutions.

39

A Wingbeat in the Wild

Long ago, on a humble wooden bridge nestled over a gentle stream, sat an old sage with his eager pupil, Happy Knuckles. They dipped their feet into the cool, flowing waters, allowing the ripples to tell tales of the unseen world beneath. Happy Knuckles, always the curious one, turned to the sage with a shimmer of curiosity in his eyes.

"Master," he began, trying to probe the wrinkled vaults of wisdom, "Have you ever fancied wealth?" The sage merely shook his head. "It's but a bed of thorns," he murmured.

Undeterred, Happy Knuckles ventured further, "How about a house full of sons, a lineage to carry forth your name?" Again, the sage declined. "Each heart you hold holds a tempest of its own," he said softly.

"But surely, a long life is a bounty everyone seeks," urged Happy Knuckles, with a youthful gleam that knew not the taste of time. The sage sighed, a sigh that carried with it the weight and wisdom of years. "Longevity often dances with frailty," he gently reminded.

At that very moment, as if on cue, a quail rustled from the embrace of nearby foliage, and soared over their heads with wings that cut through the air in poetic freedom. The sage, with a face carved with serenity, pointed towards the sky. "Ah, to be that quail, to caress the skies, to be cradled by the arms of the wild. That," he whispered with a faint smile, "is a treasure untold."

The mere simplicity of being, of blending with the unadorned rhythm of nature, was the sage's heart's desire. The trappings of wealth, the tumult of familial bonds, and the creeping shadow of age were but fleeting clouds against the vast, unyielding sky of existence.

Lessons:

The sage, in his humble wish to embody the freedom of a quail, tells us towards a truth oft-forgotten. There exists a profound serenity in simplicity, a silent joy in merging with the natural cadence of life. Much like the calm waters they sat by, life too has a rhythm, a flow that seeks not the tumult of possession, but the gentle caress of existence.

We live in times where our self-worth is often tied to the scales of material achievement, where the cacophony of modern existence drowns the simple joys of being. It takes but a moment of quiet reflection, a silent, earnest dialogue with the self to discern the true treasure of life. In the gentle rustle of leaves, in the cool kiss of the breeze, in the soft murmur of the stream, lies a wealth untold, a joy untouched by time.

40

The Deer King's Gift

Once upon a time, not far from the bustling city of Varanasi, a stretch of lush forest was home to elegant herds of deer. The golden Banyan King, with his majestic antlers and emerald eyes, led one of these herds with grace and wisdom. Nearby, another herd was led by the equally beautiful Branch King, who often sought advice from the Banyan King.

The human king of Varanasi had a peculiar craving for fresh venison. Every day, after attending to royal matters, he'd head north with his hunting party, disrupting the lives of the local villagers. The daily hunts forced farmers, bakers, and other villagers to leave their work and assist in chasing deer into the open for the king.

One smart young girl among the villagers suggested herding the deer into the king's enclosed garden so they wouldn't need to interrupt their work daily. The idea was welcomed and soon, the Banyan and Branch herds found themselves entrapped in the royal enclosure.

The human king was thrilled with the idea and even made an exception for the two remarkable golden deer, sparing them from being hunted. But the daily hunt for the king's meal turned the peaceful enclosure into a site of fear and chaos for the deer.

Troubled by the daily mayhem, Banyan King proposed a system to minimize the harm. He suggested that a lottery system could determine a single sacrificial deer daily, from either herd, making the process less chaotic. The idea was accepted and implemented.

One day, a pregnant doe from the Branch herd was chosen. Distraught, she approached Branch King for mercy, but he turned her down fearing others might demand similar exemptions. Desperate, she approached Banyan King who, without a second thought, offered himself in her stead.

When the human king discovered this sacrificial act, he was deeply moved. The Banyan King's act of compassion reminded the human king about the virtues of kindness, sacrifice, and leadership. He declared an end to the hunting of deer, vowing to give up meat altogether. Thus, the two herds were released back to their serene forests, living peacefully ever after.

Lessons:
The tale of the Banyan Deer brings forth a myriad of valuable lessons for adults. It's not just a story about the humane and wise decisions of the Banyan King but a reflection on the kind of leadership that's often missing in today's world. A leader's role isn't just about managing, but embodying virtues that safeguard the welfare of all, even at a personal cost.

Similarly, the human king's change of heart demonstrates a willingness to learn and evolve, a quality that often gets overshadowed by the rigidity and routine of modern adult life. The story invites us to reflect on our daily choices, the impact they have on others, and the environment. It moves us to consider a more compassionate stance in our interactions and decisions, a reminder that's much needed in today's fast-paced, often indifferent world.

Moreover, the initiative of the young girl illustrates how simple yet innovative solutions can come from the most unexpected quarters, encouraging adults to stay open to ideas, no matter where they originate from.

Lastly, the narrative highlights the importance of community, cooperation, and the common good, values that seem to be fading in a world dominated by individual pursuits. The tale beckons a return to compassionate community living, where the good of many takes precedence over the desires of a few. Through the lens of two kings - one human, one deer - we're gently reminded of the enduring values of kindness, sacrifice, and the transformative power of empathy.

41

The Unexpected Reflections

Once upon a time, in a kingdom known for its enchanting landscapes, Princess Lavender and the wise Sage decided to take a stroll in the royal wildlife preserve just beyond the palace gardens. Princess Lavender, known far and wide for her charm, was the gem of the kingdom.

During their serene walk, they stumbled upon a peaceful pond nestled between gentle hills. Intrigued by the calmness of the waters, Princess Lavender leaned over to catch a glimpse of the playful trout swimming underneath the gleaming surface.

However, upon noticing her reflection, the trout darted away into the depths of the pond in haste.

Further along, they encountered a heron, poised gracefully by the pond's edge, its keen eyes fixed on the shimmering waters below, waiting for a chance to nab its lunch. But as it sensed the presence of the princess, it hastily flapped its wings, soaring into the clear blue sky, leaving behind a ripple on the water's surface.

As they continued their stroll, they came across a majestic stag sipping quietly from the pond. The stag, upon lifting its head and spotting the princess, leaped in surprise and raced into the thick foliage, disappearing from sight.

With a tinge of sadness in her eyes, Princess Lavender turned to the sage, "Why do they flee from me? Am I not gentle to behold?"

The sage, with a reassuring smile, responded, "Princess, your beauty is unmatched in the kingdom, yet beauty is a realm where perceptions vary. What charms one may startle another, for the eyes see, but the mind interprets."

Lessons:

In this tale, there's a gentle nudge towards the understanding that the perception of beauty and other qualities are subjective and may vary widely among different beings. In our modern world, the rush for acceptance and validation often blinds us to this simple truth. Not everyone will perceive us in the way we perceive ourselves or in the way we desire to be perceived. And that's alright. It's an invitation to cultivate patience and understanding, to respect the varying perceptions and feelings of others even if they don't align with our expectations.

In a world increasingly interconnected yet individually diverse, embracing such understanding allows for a harmonious coexistence. Whether in personal relationships or broader societal contexts, recognizing the lens through which others view the world, with all its biases and interpretations, can foster a climate of respect, kindness, and acceptance.

42

The Chatty Voyager

Once upon a time in a beautiful lake nestled within the gentle embrace of the Himalayas, two youthful geese befriended a tortoise. They found joy in the serene waters embellished by blooming lilies and lotus, under a canopy of whispering trees. Among the rocky bays of the lake, they stumbled upon a tortoise, a chatterbox of a creature, yet with a heart full of kindness.

Through the bright summer and autumn, they reveled in each other's company until winter loomed, signaling the time for the geese to migrate to warmer climes. The trio was drowned in sorrow at the thought of parting. The tortoise wished to tag along but acknowledged his slow pace would be a hurdle.

The geese hatched a plan. They knew of the tortoise's iron grip, so they suggested a scheme where the tortoise could clench onto a stick carried by the geese as they flew to their winter haven. The only condition was that the tortoise must keep silent to maintain his grip. Thrilled, the tortoise agreed.

The day arrived and with the tortoise holding firm to the stick, they took flight. Soaring above the village, they became a spectacle for the villagers below, especially the children who were in awe of this unusual sight. In the excitement, a child yelled a question to the tortoise, inquiring about the bizarre spectacle. Without a second thought, the tortoise, filled with joy, responded, losing his grip and plummeting to his unfortunate demise. His geese friends circled back with hope but found their friend lifeless, a victim of his own loquacity. With heavy hearts, they continued on their migration, learning a harsh lesson about the perils of not heeding important advice even amidst exciting or provoking circumstances.

Lessons:

Reflecting on this tale, we see how even the most enchanting of adventures could possess lessons veiled in tragedy. The tortoise's excitement led to a forgetfulness that cost him dearly, a reminder to us that in the hustle and chatter of today's fast-paced world, a moment of silence, of pause, can sometimes be our savior.

In a time where responses are often impulsive, triggered by the rush of social media notifications or the pressure to react, pausing could be the thread of grace that keeps our world harmonious. The tale also imparts a lesson on the essence of following through on well-intended advice especially when it is for our good.

The narrative reflects the warmth and friendship Charlie Mackesy depicts in his works, showing that even in the simplest of interactions, there's depth and learning. The simple act of pausing, reflecting before reacting, or speaking is an art lost in modern chaos. Revisiting it could not only save us from unforeseen perils but enrich our relationships and experiences in a world that increasingly forgets the value of a thoughtful pause amidst the ceaseless chatter.

43

The Timely Rescue

Once upon a time, in a modest village, there lived a wise old sage who fell upon tough times. With scarce food and resources, the sage decided to approach the local wealthy landowner, Mr. Bracket, in hopes of receiving some aid.

On reaching Mr. Bracket's mansion, the sage politely asked, "Good sir, could you spare a small bag of grains to help me through these trying times?"

Mr. Bracket, with a slight frown, responded, "I am afraid my granary is a bit depleted at the moment. However, in six months, I'll be collecting my dues from the villagers and will be able to give you a hundred gold coins then."

The sage sighed and shared a small incident he experienced on his way there. "On my journey here, I stumbled upon a small golden fish stranded in a puddle, desperate to reach the nearby river. It pleaded, 'Could you help me reach the water before I perish?' I responded to the fish, 'I'm in a bit of a rush now, but how about I return next week and dig a channel from the river to your puddle? That way, you'll have ample water.' But alas, by then, the fish would have already succumbed."

With a pause, the sage looked into Mr. Bracket's eyes, "A hundred gold coins might sound generous, but they serve me no purpose if I am not alive to receive them."

Mr. Bracket's face softened as he understood the sage's metaphor. He ordered his servants to provide the sage with enough grains to last him several months.

Lessons:

The essence of this tale emboldens the immediacy of acting with a compassionate heart, especially when aid is sought in desperate times. It's an ageless narrative that rings true even in today's world.

These days, promises of future help are often tossed around, yet the urgency of now is overlooked. This story pushes adults to acknowledge and act upon the requests for help they encounter daily, be it from a family member, a friend, or a stranger. The fusion of patience and timely action, as illustrated by the sage's analogy, forms a balance we all need to strive for.

When Mr. Bracket chose to act immediately, he did not just save a life but also learned a vital lesson in empathy and responsiveness. Such a lesson is an invitation for us to cultivate a readiness to aid and a reminder that the impact of our actions, or inactions, is felt most in the present moment.

Moreover, the narrative calls for an earnest reflection on how we can move beyond mere promises to engage in actions that reflect our shared humanity. Whether it's helping someone in distress or simply being there for others when they need us, the opportunity to exhibit kindness and understanding is ever-present.

44

The Chronicles of Unlikely Friendship

Once upon a time, nestled within the peaceful lap of the mighty Himalayas, stood a colossal banyan tree. This wasn't just any tree, but a rendezvous spot for three unique friends—a partridge, a monkey, and an elephant. They had shared a bond since memory served, but of late, cracks appeared in their camaraderie, manifesting as petty quarrels and misunderstandings. Fearing the demise of their cherished friendship, they resolved to add a hint of structure to their relationship. They believed a hint of hierarchy, determining the elder among them to lead, could mend the fraying threads of their companionship, for that mirrored the world's way.

Their towering companion, the banyan tree, became the judge of age. The partridge posed a question to the elephant, "Can you recall the size of the banyan when you first saw it?"

After a thoughtful pause, the elephant reminisced, "I remember stepping over it as a calf, feeling its young foliage tickle my belly."

The inquiry then swung to the monkey, who chirped, "Oh, I recall leaning down to nibble the tender shoots of what was a mere shrub back then, while seated on the ground."

Lastly, the partridge shared its tale, "I carry a tale from a time before this tree sprouted from the earth. I had feasted on the fruits of another majestic banyan across the river, and flew over here, leaving the seeds behind in my wake. This grand tree is a descendant of those very seeds."

The testimony led the monkey and the elephant to a unanimous nod, acknowledging the partridge as the eldest, the newfound leader among them. With a newfound respect, they agreed to heed the partridge's counsel. Embracing her role, the partridge suggested a pact of mutual respect and graciousness, vanishing the seeds of discord that threatened their union, ensuring the sunset each day on their undying friendship.

Lessons:

In this simple yet profound tale, the enduring friendship among diverse beings shines a light on the significance of patience, understanding, and respect in nurturing relationships. The modern sphere often witnesses relationships straining under the weight of ego and misunderstanding, much like the trio before their pact. Their thoughtful introspection and willingness to evolve remind us that the essence of any relationship lies in mutual respect, patience, and the ability to value each other's individuality while learning and growing together. This narrative encourages adults to take a step back, cherish the existing bonds, and navigate through misunderstandings with a gentle, open heart, much like our three companions under the banyan's shade.

45

Flight Lessons

Once, in a time much simpler than today, there lived an old sage, wise from the years etched onto his face. With his faithful student, who went by the unusual name of Pickled Fencepost, they wandered through the buzzing streets of a city whose heartbeat from the royal palace that stood at its center. The palace was a grand edifice, veiled by a towering wall and guarded by men of valor, protecting the unseen ruler nestled within its belly.

One afternoon, as the sun cast long shadows on the cobblestone streets, Pickled Fencepost, looking at the fortified palace, asked with the innocence of the unseasoned, "Why do people need kings?" Before the sage could respond, a sudden symphony of honking drew their gaze upwards. A formation of geese, like a moving arrow, etched a path across the clear blue sky, casting fleeting shadows over the opulent palace roofs.

The sage, with a hint of a smile, said, "Look at the geese, dear Fencepost. In their orderly voyage, each takes a turn at the helm, leading the way through the unseen air currents. Then, as if by silent agreement, they rotate, allowing another to take the lead. There's no crown among them, yet they flow in harmony, knowing innately what to do. They don't require a king to guide them on what to believe or where to remain loyal."

As they ambled on, the reflection on shared leadership lingered between them, swirling with the dust kicked up by their wandering feet.

Lessons:

Now, the tale of the geese over the royal palace offers a nugget of wisdom. It talks about shared leadership, an ethos much needed in our modern world often entangled in the wrangling for power and control. In simpler terms, it's like a group project at work where each member takes a turn leading a portion of the project. By doing so, not only is the burden of leadership shared, but it also allows for a diverse range of ideas to flow, creating a richer outcome. The geese, in their natural wisdom, mirror the collaborative spirit, a beacon of effortless teamwork and shared responsibility.

In a world where hierarchy often defines the order, rekindling the simplicity and effectiveness of shared leadership could foster a more harmonious and egalitarian society. It could mend the rigid structures of corporate ladders, inviting a breeze of fresh perspectives. Just like the geese, sharing the sky and easing each other's flight, humans too can find a balance between leading and following, nurturing a culture of mutual respect and collective growth. Through this tale, one may glean that true leadership isn't about clinging to power, but about fostering a space where every voice has the freedom to echo and be heard.

46

A Speck in the Cosmos

Once, a curious disciple named Woody shared a quiet evening with his wise mentor, under a sky filled with twinkling stars. The serenity of the moment was briefly interrupted when Woody, feeling a wave of insignificance, said, "It's remarkable how enormous the world is, and how I appear to be just a speck in this vastness."

His mentor, recognizing a teaching moment, casually replied, "Well, what does it mean to be small or large, Woody? Take for instance a fox's fur, a single strand is tiny, almost invisible. Now look up, the sky, stretching endlessly, is immense. Yet, one defines the other. Without the tiny, how would we grasp the enormity of the large? The West helps us find the East, every element, no matter its size, has its role in the grand scheme."

"There's nothing about the endless sky that makes it more significant than you or even the minuscule strand of the fox's fur. Each entity, big or small, holds its unique place, crafting the story of the universe. Your existence, the expansive sky, and the fox's fur are threads in the intricate fabric of existence, each essential to complete the picture."

This narrative moves us to reflect on the concept of significance in a boundless universe. Woody's moment of self-doubt is something we all experience. Especially in a modern era, where comparisons on social platforms might lead to feelings of inadequacy. However, every person, job, and action, no matter how minor it seems, contributes to the larger tapestry of life. Our worth isn't defined by our visibility or the grandness of our actions, but by the unique essence and integrity, we bring into our daily interactions and duties.

The modest interaction between Woody and his mentor encourages us to embrace both the vastness and the minutiae of life. It invites a kinder perspective towards ourselves and others, fostering appreciation over judgment, patience over haste, and gratitude over discontentment.

Lessons:

Today, where being 'significant' is often measured by material success or social recognition, this story serves as a gentle reminder. It beckons us to honor the inherent value in ourselves and others, urging a culture of respect and contentment, much needed in our modern day.

47

A Cave Tale in the Pouring Rain

Once upon a time, near the bustling city of Varanasi, there lay a thick, wild forest. The rains in this region were relentless, often showering the woods for days on end. During one such torrential downpour, an old black monkey found himself trudging through the wet underbrush, desperately searching for shelter. His fur was soaked, and his bones ached with cold. Hours of tiresome search led him to a snug cave tucked away behind a rocky outcrop. At the entrance sat a young red monkey, nestled comfortably away from the rain.

The black monkey approached, hopeful. He thought, "Surely, this young one will invite an elder like me to share this warm refuge." He waited patiently at the entrance, eyes meeting the red monkeys, waiting for an invite. But the red monkey turned a blind eye, acting as though the black monkey was invisible.

This lack of courtesy infuriated the old monkey, prompting him to devise a little ruse. He puffed up his belly, feigning fullness, and exclaimed, "Oh, the ripe figs I just feasted on were the finest, so succulent and sweet!"

Suddenly, the red monkey perked up, "Hello Uncle! You seem to have found something delicious. Are the figs nearby?"

The old monkey was quick to respond, "Oh, not far at all. I can guide you, and you'll be feasting in no time!" And so, the naive red monkey scampered off into the rain in search of the figs, while the old black monkey took refuge in the warm, dry cave.

Time passed, and eventually, the red monkey returned, wetter and colder than before, having found no figs. He realized he had been tricked. But he thought he'd give trickery a try as well. Rubbing his stomach, he said, "Thank you, Uncle, for both the shelter and the fantastic fig spot. They were delicious! Plenty left for you."

But the black monkey didn't budge, he looked straight at the young monkey and retorted, "Did you honor me when you left me in the pouring rain? Only a fool would fall for his trick. Learn to respect your elders." Disheartened and soaked to the bone, the red monkey ventured back into the rain, in search of another shelter.

Lessons:
This tale, wrapped in simple mischief and humor, serves as a soft reminder of the age-old teaching of respect and understanding between generations. It's essential, even in our modern bustling lives, to maintain a sense of decency, and respect, especially towards our elders who have traversed the path of life much longer. They offer a canopy of wisdom, much like the cave provided shelter to the monkeys from the harsh rain.

In a world that often forgets the importance of simple courtesies, this story can serve as a gentle nudge towards practicing them, cultivating a culture of respect, patience, and understanding, transcending the barriers of age and experience, akin to a warm, inviting cave amidst a relentless storm of modern complexities.

48

The Little Builders and the Big Questions

Once, in a quiet part of the woods, a wise teacher and his earnest student, named Tim, found themselves resting upon a sturdy, fallen branch. They were admiring a convoy of termites, busy transporting tiny chunks of wood back to their home. The rhythmic movement of these little builders seemed almost meditative.

"Teacher," Tim sighed, breaking the silence between them, "I find my heart heavy and my thoughts darker with each passing day. Despite my efforts, a cloud of worry hangs over me."

The wise teacher, with a gentle smile, began drawing small hurdles in the sand in the path of the termites using a slender twig. The termites, undeterred, navigated through them with grace and determination.

"Tim," the teacher began softly, "look at these tiny creatures. Notice how, no matter the hurdles, they navigate through without losing their calm, staying focused on their path. Our minds, akin to this sandy path, often find thoughts crossing over, some light, some heavy. When these thoughts cross paths continuously, they can spark a flame of worry and fear, burning our peace away. It's not about stopping these thoughts, but about letting them pass. Let them come, let them go. It's the resistance that often causes the pain."

Tim looked at the termites, then at his teacher. A subtle understanding dawned upon him.

Lessons:
This narrative subtly hints at the idea of acceptance and allowing thoughts to flow rather than resisting them. It's a gentle nudge to adults to observe, accept, and let go, much like the termites effortlessly overcoming the hurdles. This story could serve as a

reminder in today's fast-paced world, where our minds are often entangled in endless thoughts. The lesson of sailing smoothly over worries, just like termites, can bring a fresh perspective toward handling our anxieties and fears.

In a world constantly urging us to control and resolve, perhaps there's merit in letting things be, letting thoughts come and go. Just like Tim, with a little observation and patience, we might find our worries simplifying themselves, teaching us the beauty of effortless resolution.

49

A Tale of Two Fawns

Once, nestled amidst the lush greens north of the grand city of Varanasi, lived a seasoned elder deer renowned for his sage advice. He was the go-to mentor for the young fawns in his large herd. One sunny morning, his younger sister approached him with her twin fawns, expressing her desire for them to be tutored under his wise wings.

Gladly agreeing, the elder deer asked the twins to meet him the following noon for their first lesson. As the sun hovered straight above the next day, only one twin showed up, eager for wisdom.

His sibling, known for his frivolity, chose to skip the lesson for a playful dash through the woods. This pattern repeated over weeks, the earnest twin soaking up wisdom, while his brother danced through the forest's dappled sunlight.

Fate's cruel twist awaited the frolicsome twin as he found himself ensnared by a hunter's trap one afternoon. His frantic struggles only tightened the snare, cutting into his flesh. Overwhelmed by fear and pain, he trembled till the hunter arrived, ending his young life for a meal.

The news spread through the herd like wildfire, shrouding their hearts with sorrow, especially the mother and the wise uncle. Undeterred, the wise twin continued his tutelage, growing in knowledge with each passing day.

Fortune tested him too, as he found himself snared one day. Yet, his response was of calm intellect. He feigned death convincingly, fooling the hunter into releasing the snare. The moment the hunter's attention wavered, the wise twin sprinted back into the deep forest, his heart pounding with victorious adrenaline.

His return to the herd was a celebration of wisdom triumphing over adversity. His mother's tears of joy mingled with the proud eyes of the mentor who knew the value of a disciplined mind.

Lessons:

The modern world, much like the forest in our tale, is filled with unseen snares. Each choice we make could lead us either into a trap or towards liberation. Much like the frivolous twin, we often get entangled in the allure of short-term pleasures, ignoring the essential lessons that could arm us against life's adversities. The wise twin symbolizes the importance of preparedness and continuous learning which aren't merely about survival but leading a life filled with insightful decisions.

Our mentors, akin to the elder deer, play a crucial role. They hand us the compass of discernment to navigate through life's unpredictable trails. The contrasting fates of the twins shed light on the impacts of our choices and the significance of having a disciplined, educated mind. As adults, engaging in lifelong learning and seeking mentorship can be our shield against unforeseen challenges.

Just as the wise twin's calmness and intellect saved him from the hunter's snare, our collected mindfulness can free us from modern-day traps of stress, impulsive decisions, or anxiety. Through mindful living, patience, and continuous learning, we find ourselves better equipped to face life's intricacies, much like the clever fawn dancing through the woods yet aware of the earth beneath his hooves.

50

The Mighty Heart of True Happiness

In the small bustling town of Gandhara in ancient India, there was a compassionate farmer who found a companion in a young ox calf. The farmer named the ox True Happiness, raising it with a loving heart, and nurturing it like a child of his own. As time rolled on, True Happiness matured into a strong and magnificent creature, embodying power and grace.

One day, grateful for the love he'd received, True Happiness proposed a wager to the farmer. He believed he could pull a weight no other ox in the region could. He suggested they find a wealthy merchant to bet a thousand silver pieces against the strength of True Happiness to move a hundred loaded carts. The farmer, though hesitant, trusted in the heart of his dear companion and took on the wager.

The day of the challenge dawned bright and clear, with the town buzzing in anticipation. A line of a hundred loaded carts was assembled, and True Happiness was adorned with garlands, standing tall, ready to prove his might. However, as the farmer took his seat on the first cart, the weight of what was at stake crushed his spirit, replacing his calm demeanor with a storm of anxiety. He yelled harsh words, urging True Happiness to move, contrasting the gentle whispers True Happiness was accustomed to. The ox was stunned by the change in his beloved master's tone, rendering him immovable despite the shouts and the lash of a whip.

The farmer lost the wager, his heart sank, and he returned home, buried in regret. True Happiness followed him home and questioned the harsh words and actions, revealing the hurt that made him immobile. The farmer, realizing his mistake, acknowledged the deep bond they shared, understanding that his fear and greed had momentarily blinded him.

With renewed hope and understanding, the farmer approached the merchant for a rematch, doubling the wager. The merchant, smirking, agreed. The townsfolk jeered as True Happiness was once again yoked to the carts, but this time, the farmer, with a gentle voice and a tender heart, whispered words of encouragement to True Happiness. The mighty ox, heartened by the love and faith of his master, pulled the line of carts with ease, proving his might and winning the wager.

Lessons:

This simple yet profound interaction between the farmer and True Happiness paints a picture that transcends the ancient setting and finds its relevance even today. In the bustling chaos of modern life, where the stakes always seem high, fear often replaces faith, and harsh words replace gentle whispers. It reflects how tender encouragement can achieve what harshness fails to, no matter the enormity of the challenge at hand. It's a quiet reminder that the choice of words and the tone of interactions, whether with others or oneself, significantly impacts the outcomes of the endeavors undertaken.

Furthermore, the companionship between the farmer and True Happiness gently unveils the essence of trust, respect, and understanding, virtues that stand the test of time. It's a story from which adults navigating the complex terrains of modern relationships and challenges can draw comfort and wisdom. Amidst the onslaught of expectations and the pursuit of success, the essence of kind communication, trust, and acknowledgment of emotions often takes a backseat, yet these are the true drivers of meaningful successes and enduring relationships.

The Crafty Sage and the Wise Rats

Once, nestled amidst the flourishing vegetation near Varanasi, there lived a community of rats. Their leader was a remarkable rat - full of strength yet gentle, vigilant yet compassionate. Not far from their dwelling, a cunning jackal resided. He often observed the rats, but their leader was too prudent, making it impossible for the jackal to catch any. Driven by his craftiness, the jackal conceived a plan.

Aware of the rat leader's reverence for the sacred, the jackal decided to masquerade as a holy sage. He positioned himself along a trail the rats frequently traversed, stood on one leg, slightly opened his mouth, and posed his paws together facing the sun in a pose of prayer.

Upon seeing the jackal, the rat leader considered changing course. But curiosity got the better of him regarding the jackal's unusual stance. He approached cautiously, inquiring, "Mr. Jackal, may I know your name?"

"Call me Godly," replied the jackal.

"And why the stance on one leg?" asked the rat.

"Were I to stand on all four, the earth would bear my weight heavily, and I wish not to harm her," lied the jackal.

"And your mouth slightly ajar?" probed the rat.

"To breathe the air. I subsist solely on it, avoiding harm to other beings," answered the jackal deceitfully.

"And your paws held together, facing the sun?" further inquired the rat.

"To honor and acknowledge the sun, the beacon of life," claimed the jackal deceitfully.

Touched by the apparent righteousness, the rat believed his community could glean wisdom from the jackal. Hence, the daily visits to the jackal began. However, every departure saw one less rat return, as the jackal stealthily caught the last rat in line, satisfying his hunger.

Soon, the wise rat leader noticed the dwindling numbers. The onset of this mishap coincided with the visits to the jackal. He deduced the faux sage's malevolent actions. The next visit saw the leader taking up the rear. As anticipated, the jackal pounced but found himself faced with the defiant, ready leader. A fierce resistance ensued, summoning the entire rat community to their leader's defense. They chased away the deceitful jackal far into the woods, ensuring safety once more.

As they tread back, the leader pondered, "Sometimes, what adorns a veil of sanctity often masks malevolence."

Lessons:

The story underscores the importance of discernment and vigilance, even when faced with seemingly benign or holy personas. In an era where misinformation and deceit are rampant, often veiled in the guise of authority or sanctity, it's essential to employ discernment. The sagacious rat leader in our tale reminds us to always observe, question, and analyze situations, particularly when anomalies arise. This vigilance, coupled with a ready community, can safeguard against malevolent forces attempting to harm or mislead. Like the wise rat leader, it's crucial to remain grounded in reality, not swept away by mere appearances, ensuring the well-being of our community and ourselves.

The Ape's Heartfelt Rescue

Once, nestled amidst the Himalayas, a farmer found himself stranded. After losing his oxen, he wandered off into the wilderness and soon enough, he found himself at the precipice of a deep cavern. His misstep led him to plummet down, saved only by a pool of water below. For five days, he struggled, living off a few fallen fruits and the mercy of the pool's water.

On the sixth morning, a gentle black ape discovered him while foraging. Upon hearing the farmer's plight, compassion surged within the ape, promising help. The ape devised the only way out was to have the farmer cling onto his back while he climbed out of the abyss. The ordeal was grueling, but the ape's resolve didn't flinch.

Having reached safer ground, the ape, exhausted, asked the farmer to keep a watch while he rested before they journeyed onward. However, as the ape slept, a sinister thought danced around the farmer's mind. "With the ape's meat, I shall regain strength and find my way home," he thought. He found a hefty stone, aimed at the ape, and hurled it. But, fatigue hampered his aim, only startling the ape awake.

Upon realization, sadness washed over the ape's face. Yet, instead of wrath, the ape displayed a profound understanding of the darker incline of human desperation. He walked the farmer to a point where the path home was clear, advising him to walk ahead as trust was now a fragile thread between them.

As the farmer trudged his way home, the ape's final words resonated, "Your act may haunt you, as kindness begets kindness, and malice, malice."

Lessons:

This story is a mirror of the values of compassion, trust, and the repercussions of desperate actions in dire circumstances. We live in a world where help might come from the most unexpected quarters, akin to the gentle ape in the narrative. In our haste or desperation, overlooking or abusing such assistance can lead to a chain of regrettable actions, much like the farmer's fleeting sinister thought.

Being cognizant of the weight of our actions, especially when shown kindness, is essential. The tapestry of trust and mutual respect is delicate and once torn, it's arduous to mend. The story impels us to reflect on the virtue of gratitude and the consequential harmony or discord stemming from our actions, a lesson pertinent to navigating the complex social fabric of our contemporary lives.

Moreover, the narrative extends a broader stroke on the essence of compassion, not merely as a virtue but as a bedrock of co-existence. The ape's unyielding resolve to help, even when faced with betrayal, paints a poignant picture of selfless compassion, a trait that holds profound relevance in fostering a kinder society amidst a world grappling with polarities.

Thus, embracing gratitude and compassion, and understanding the far-reaching impacts of our actions, particularly in testing times, could pave a path towards a more empathetic and understanding society.

Conclusion

As we wrap up our journey through these Zen stories, it's like we've been on a quiet, thoughtful walk through a forest full of life lessons. From the very first story of the boastful beetle to the last heartfelt rescue by an ape, every tale has nudged us to look at life a bit differently.

These stories, though filled with playful animals and simple situations, carry big lessons. They invite us to take a pause, look around, and soak in the simple yet profound lessons scattered in our daily lives.

We met characters who showed us what patience, kindness, and respect look like, even when faced with challenges. For example, the humble wanderer's story is a gentle reminder to appreciate what we have, and the playful tormenter gives us a sneak peek into the power of patience.

In today's world, where being busy is a badge of honor, these stories are a breath of fresh air. They remind us to slow down, to not let anger drive us, and to face life's bumps with a smile, much like the characters in "Morning Nuts and Monkey Business" and "The Sly Spearman and the Wise Deer."

Life might get tough, but as the stories show, with a sprinkle of courage, a dash of gratitude, and a big heart full of integrity, we can make our journey meaningful. It's not about never falling, but about getting back up, learning from our missteps, and moving forward with a smile, just like the determined characters in "The Dance of Fortune" and "The Boozy Beak Brigade."

Each story is a gentle tap on the shoulder, a friendly reminder to carry these simple yet impactful lessons as we step out into the bustling world. As we turn over the last page of this book, the real adventure begins - taking these lessons off the pages and bringing them to life in our daily interactions.

So, as we step into the hustle and bustle of our lives, let's carry with us the simplicity, the laughter, and the lessons from these tales. Let's sprinkle a bit of patience, kindness, and gratitude as we go along, making our world a bit more like the creative yet wise world of these Zen stories.

9 789693 292770